ABSENT FRIEND

Laura and Martyn Lee

Sponsored by
The Cambridge Pet Crematorium
and
CPC Petrest

HENSTON

First published 1992

© Henston Ltd, 1992

ISBN 1 85054 089 6

Henston Ltd, The Chequers, 2 Church Street, High Wycombe, Bucks, England

Printed and bound by Brier Press Ltd, HighWycombe, Bucks

Cover design by CBA & Associates Ltd

Cover photograph by Judith Howell, shows Irving and Holly, two life-long friends

HENSTON

Contents

Foreword and Preface iv

Man and his animals 1

Love hurts 11

A sudden death 25

What to tell the children 36

Pets and the elderly 54

Euthanasia 63

The final resting place 77

Loss without a body 91

Filling the gap 105

Do pets grieve? 118

Obituaries 125

Appendix 1: Pet loss – the facts 132

Appendix 2: Pet charities 139

Acknowledgements

Henston gratefuly acknowledges the support received from The Cambridge Pet Crematorium and CPC Petrest which has made the production of this book possible.

Our special thanks also to Gareth Osborne for his encouragement and help with this publication.

Jim Evans, Editor

Foreword

The man coming into my office was so big he had to lower his head through the doorway. Strong arms cradled a box in a loving way and I went forward to help, sensing that he might stumble.

'Please can you cremate Kal... for me.' The name was lost in a flood of tears. I took the box and was surprised at how light it was. June, my receptionist, sat the gentleman down and gave him a cup of tea.

The sad figure, now sitting with head buried in hands, was but a shadow of his former self. I gently took the box containing his beloved pet through to the crematorium and opened it. I stopped in amazement to find, curled round inside, a python.

A strange pet, you might think, but after 10 years of individually cremating the loved pets of thousands of owners, I am no longer surprised by the love that exists between man and his animals. I have come to realise that at the sad time of any pet's death, grief is just as real and a great deal less understood than when a close human friend or relative is lost.

Bereavement affects us all in different ways, but regardless of colour, creed or class, our tears are the same.

Because of my close involvement with bereaved people, I had no hesitation in accepting when I was asked to write a foreword to this book.

As I read Laura and Martyn's thoughts, I became convinced that they know their subject and handle it in a most sympathetic and caring way. Here I found all the things I had ever wanted to express and as I continued through the book, memories of countless wonderful people and their animals that I have met over the years came flooding back:

- The lady from St Neots who wanted to sit with her dead dog for a while, just remembering how it used to be.
- The 40-year-old parrot which had spent his years flying freely around the family home, going into his cage only to use the toilet.
- The pony that was brought to my crematorium for euthanasia. I remember so well taking him for a walk around our gardens of remembrance; he was 41 years old!

A memory I will always treasure is that of the gentleman who went sea fishing every week with his dog. After the day at sea he would bring his small boat home and 20 yards from shore the dog would jump into the water and swim ashore to await his master on the jetty. With the boat safely tied up, they would walk home together. When this gentleman lost his dog, he knew exactly what he was going to do once the cremation was completed. He took the ashes to sea, fished all day and then made for home. Just 20 yards from shore, he scattered the ashes in the place where his dog used to jump into the water. That was a very special and personal place for that gentleman, and one which will always revive his memories of those happy times.

Owners never believe that they are going to lose their pet – so they are seldom prepared for the loss. Patch, my own dog, was fading quickly and on my vet's advice I reluctantly accepted that the time had come for euthanasia. But Patch rallied and we agreed that I would take him home. I remember what a problem that seemed, when I realised that I had come by motorbike, but I tucked Patch into the front of my zip-up suit and took him home to Ilford with his head and front paws sticking out the front.

As I rode home I thought of how he had come to join our family. He had been abandoned and was going to be destroyed because the previous owners said he bit children. Well, Patch bit no one in my house, and throughout his life was a beloved family member. He grew up with our children to become a very close friend of mine who never left my side.

When we first opened our crematorium and installed the equipment, I was told by the council planners that the chimney had to be painted brown, in keeping with the rest of the building. I climbed the ladder very uncertainly, being less than keen on heights. As I reached the top, I found I was not alone – Patch was right behind me! My fear evaporated as I tried to hold the brush, paint and Patch and return to the safety of solid ground.

I eventually lost Patch in 1989 when he was over 18 years old. His ashes now lie in our gardens of remembrance by the tree he always watered. I talk to him regularly as I walk around the gardens and thoughts of him still come back to me. Time is a great healer and I can now smile at his antics and that bike ride home. Before losing him, my role as a bereavement counsellor was just a job; since then it has become a crusade.

If you think you are on your own as you read this book, please be assured that you are not. There are many who feel the way you do and we see many of them here at the crematorium every week.

For those who have lost a pet there will always remain the memories...for me there will always be Patch.

This book will be of help to *all* pet owners and will, I hope, provide comfort to those who grieve the loss of a well-loved pet.

Clive Jackman
Cambridge Pet Crematorium

Preface

We started to research the effects of pet loss because as a voluntary bereavement counsellor and a vet, we became aware that owners did not realise that it was *normal* to grieve for a pet. As a consequence we carried out a survey on British attitudes to pet loss and researched just how people coped when they lost a pet. The decision to turn the research into a book was made when Benson, our nine-year-old cat, died quite unexpectedly of cancer. At that point we felt we truly understood our subject.

This book is for anyone who loves, lives with or works with animals – even non-pet owners may find the text enlightening. Pet owners can use the book as a guide to coping with the numerous problems associated with pet loss, including how to prepare for the inevitable occurrence of pet death. The text examines the individual needs of children and the elderly, and it looks at the difficult question of euthanasia. Practical issues such as what to do with the pet's body, how to deal with a pining pet and what to do if the family pet goes missing are all addressed in *Absent Friend*.

However, the main purpose of this book is to give all those people who truly love animals the permission they need, and yet which is so often lacking, to grieve for their faithful animal friends.

We would like to thank the following for their encouragement and support in writing this book: Celia Haddon, Andrew Edney, both our families, Yvonne and Bernadette, but most of all the people who took part in the research and have shared with us the pain of loving and losing a pet.

Finally, this book is dedicated to Benson, Honey and Fat Ada – and all the other pets we have owned.

Laura and Martyn Lee

Chapter 1

Man and his animals

When the body that lived at your single will,
With its whimper of welcome, is stilled (how still!)
When the spirit that answered your every mood
Is gone – wherever it goes – for good,
You will discover how much you care,
And you will give your heart to a dog to tear.

Rudyard Kipling, **The power of the dog**

Pets through the ages

Why we form attachments to pets

Pets and the family

Positive aspects of pet ownership

Pets and the sick and disabled

Working dogs

Pets through the ages

'I am not a man who cries easily,but picking up her bone and her rubber ball, her food and water dishes, I cried as I haven't cried since childhood. I'm glad my wife wasn't there to see me cry that way because I would have had to stop then and the hurt within me would have been worse.'

These words, in *A letter to the man who killed my dog* by Richard Joseph, typify the feelings of grief that many pet owners experience when they lose a much loved pet.

In some cases people take the relationship they share with a pet for granted until that relationship is severed. Thus, when a pet dies many people are surprised and sometimes embarrassed by their feelings of grief. Grieving for any loss in your life is a natural, healthy and acceptable reaction to that loss.

MAN AND HIS ANIMALS

Examining the role of animals throughout history and the bond that develops between a pet and its owner helps to provide a deeper understanding of why we grieve for the loss of a pet.

It's commonly assumed that the role of animals as pets is a relatively recent and Western phenomenon. In reality pet ownership probably predates the development of farming and the domestication of animals.

European explorers coming into contact with modern day Stone Age civilisations have reported evidence of pet ownership. A vast variety of animals were kept as pets by these people, a fact which casts doubt on the theory that man first used animals for work rather than for companionship.

Naturally there is no written record of when man first kept pets but archaeologists have found evidence in North America of dogs living with man as long ago as 30,000 BC. In Israel the 14,000-year-old remains of a man's body were found buried with those of a dog, the man's hand had been placed on the dog's shoulder.

Cats probably owe their domestication to their ability to catch rats and mice in the grain stores of ancient Egypt. The first evidence of cat ownership dates from around 9000 BC. As cats became domesticated they were associated with the Egyptian goddess Bast. When Bast was promoted to become the most important Egyptian goddess, the cat experienced a parallel rise in sacred status. Egyptian cats were protected by law and the death penalty awaited anyone who harmed or killed one.

Translations of Egyptian records have shown that if a cat died its owners would express their grief by shaving off their hair and eyebrows and mourning publicly for many months afterwards. Recently archaeologists have unearthed a vast cemetery containing 80,000 mummified cats, each with its own mummified mouse in case it became hungry in the afterlife.

The export of cats from Egypt was strictly limited but the Phoenicians managed to smuggle some out and sell them to the Romans. The Romans gradually exported them all over their Empire, including to Britain.

The Romans and Greeks were enthusiastic pet-owners; Nero made his horse a senator, and Alexander the Great appointed his horse, Bucephalus, a general. Many rich Romans kept large menageries to impress their friends. Dogs and cats were frequently kept as pets; they are often mentioned in contemporary literature and portrayed in wall paintings and mosaics.

During the Dark Ages, when most people lived on the land and were in daily contact with animals, the entire rural economy was based on exploiting animals for food and work. As a result, people regarded animals as servants or slaves and any concern for their welfare was discouraged. Only the upper classes had the time and money to keep animals for companionship and sport.

It was at this time that various animals came to be associated with witchcraft. Dogs, cats and other species were frequently accused of being witches' 'familiars'. The Black Death, in the 14th century, led to the rehabilitation of the cat as a domestic pet as soon as it was realised that the disease was being spread by rats.

The Industrial Revolution and associated movement of populations from the countryside into towns led to an increased interest in country life and pet ownership. As standards of living rose, more and more people were able to afford to keep a pet and pet ownership was no longer the preserve of the upper classes.

The modern concept of pet ownership dates from the late 1940s. It was at this time that people began to allow their pets to live indoors in close proximity to themselves. Recently the reduction in family size and increased personal mobility has meant that more people live alone or in small groups. The presence of a pet has consequently assumed an increased importance in the lives of us all.

Why we form attachments to pets

Whilst it is possible to own a pet simply for the enjoyment of keeping it, the majority of pet owners develop a sense of attachment to their pet which strengthens throughout the years of ownership. A pet provides owners with a sense of being needed and valued. It can provide love, devotion, companionship and non-judgmental, non-critical acceptance. A pet is uninfluenced by the status and success or failure of its owner. It will be glad to see you arrive and sad to see you leave.

One reason it is possible to become so attached to dogs and cats is that they possess a comprehensive repertoire of body language that makes it easy to interpret their moods and wants.

Occasionally the strength of attachment is so strong that it can subject the owner to major inconveniences. Owners may refuse to leave an animal when they go away on holiday or they may tolerate serious lapses in behaviour because they feel morally responsible for their pet.

The main reason we form attachments, however, is that humans are social animals and genetically programmed to form attachments, especially where there is a degree of dependency involved.

❏ Different kinds of attachment

There are many factors that can affect how closely you may become attached to your pet. These include how you came by your pet, how intimately you share your life with it, how long you have owned it and the experiences you have shared.

Rescued pets

The circumstances surrounding the acquisition of a pet can affect the depth of the bond which develops. When an animal has been rescued and nursed back to health a deep attachment may form. Also if a pet has suffered a chronic illness needing intensive nursing then the owner will feel very close to the pet and feel responsible for its future welfare.

Associations with the past

Another important factor which can influence the strength of attachment between a pet and its owner are the circumstances when the pet was acquired. In the case of a person who has recently suffered a major loss, a pet may provide the comfort and solace that is needed at that time and the resulting bond may be very strong indeed.

Pets and the family

❏ Adults

Pets can fill a number of roles in our lives, namely sibling, partner, child or friend.

Generally most people are attached to their pets and many pets are treated as members of the family whose wants and needs are taken into consideration when family decisions are being made. Adults tend to treat pets as childlike family members. There is nothing wrong with this because, although we treat them as if they were children, we know that they are really animals.

People who live alone, who may find the company of other humans somewhat lacking, may well invest a great deal of emotional energy in a relationship with a pet. They are likely to be devastated by grief and loneliness when their pet dies. This is largely because they may have regarded their pet as a substitute adult or child. This relationship is healthy provided that the owner doesn't become increasingly isolated from human society. It is worth noting that not all people who live alone are lonely and that many lonely people would not consider a pet a satisfactory substitute for human companionship.

Couples who remain childless either through choice or circumstances often become closely bonded to their pets. In some cases the pets are child substitutes, but not always. Some couples who choose not to have children feel very strongly that their pets are not child substitutes and they remain very happy with their domestic arrangements.

Young couples often acquire a pet before they decide to start a family. This doesn't automatically mean that the pet is a child substitute – it can be a convenient focus for a shared desire to nurture something. Naturally in some cases it may be a first step towards starting a family.

The role of animals as child substitutes is overstated. The majority of pet-owning households are families with children. Fewer than 9% of dogs and 14% of cats live in childless households. The roles of pets in these families are multiple and complex. Without doubt, the presence of a pet is beneficial to the whole family; it bridges the generation gap by a shared interest in the welfare of the animal.

As children grow up and leave home, mothers can often be left feeling redundant and needing a new purpose in life. In this situation a pet can fill the gap left by the departure of the children and restore the mother's role as a carer.

❏ Children

The relationship between pets and children has been studied carefully for many years. It is a relationship that changes significantly as children grow older. The important role of pets in children's lives is hardly surprising when you consider that most children are bombarded with images of animals from the moment they are born. Animals feature heavily in toys, books, pictures, soft furnishings and television programmes.

Pet animals have a number of qualities that make them important to children. Most animals are conveniently soft, warm and accommodating when the child needs comfort. Children find it easy to form a relationship with a pet and these relationships help children to form relationships with people. All pets have a vital role to play as a substitute friend or sibling. Young children include their pets in imaginary adventures, often the pet is imagined to do things that the child is forbidden or unable to do.

Naturally pets make ideal confidants for children to tell their problems to because they can't give away any secrets and they can't criticise. Looking after a pet enables a child to develop important social skills and promotes a feeling of pride and self-esteem in the young owner. The presence of a pet in a household can also provide an important sense of security.

In all cases parents should supervise the care and welfare of the pet and set clear boundaries of intimacy with the pet.It is also vital to be aware of the need to ensure the child's safety.

❏ The elderly

Pets are also important to the elderly, especially those who live alone or those who find themselves in a situation where they appear to be losing their independence, their health and their family and friends.

The presence of a pet not only provides companionship but it can greatly improve the owner's chances of meeting other people. The need to care for a pet provides a vital impetus to ensure that elderly people look after themselves too.

In many cases the pet forms an important link with friends and relatives who are no longer alive. The effect of losing a pet with such strong sentimental value can be very profound.

If elderly people have to go into sheltered accommodation and are not allowed to take their pet with them, the loss of the pet can lead to great distress and make the trauma of the move quite unbearable.

Positive aspects of pet ownership

It is generally thought that pet ownership makes you healthier. Certainly research has shown that pet owners recover from illness more quickly than other people. Current thought is that pets offer seven main benefits.

- All pets act as companions and help prevent loneliness.
- Looking after a pet requires a certain degree of physical activity, which is beneficial to the owner.
- Watching pets playing helps to keep people mentally alert.
- Pets, especially dogs, give a feeling of security. Studies have shown that the sound of a barking dog actively discourages burglars.
- Pets are a constant source of affection and physical contact.
- Looking after a pet helps owners take their minds off their own problems.

Animals can be beneficial even if no attachment exists between a person and an animal. Fish tanks in dentists' waiting rooms have been found to help reduce patients' blood pressure and make them less nervous. This effect is probably due to man's instinctive reliance on nearby animals as sensitive danger alarms; if nearby animals are relaxed it seems that we instinctively assume that there is no immediate danger and relax too.

You only have to compare the atmosphere in a doctor's waiting room with that in your local vet's to realise that a common interest in animals enables complete strangers to enjoy a pleasant conversation without stress.

Research has shown that people walking their dogs have a much greater chance of talking to someone than people walking on their own. Even if you're house-bound, owning a pet is a reason for more people to visit you. Some elderly dog owners are unable to take their dogs for walks but they are often helped by young volunteers who not only exercise the dog but also provide some company for the owner.

The presence of a pet appears to make it easier for strangers to judge the character of the owner. In general owning a dog makes you seem more approachable, often the pet does the approaching for you and in no time at all you may be discussing your pet with a stranger.

Politicians and famous people are well aware of the advantages of being seen as a pet owner and are frequently photographed accompanied by a faithful family pet.

Pets and the sick and disabled

It has been accepted for centuries that animals are beneficial in the lives of sick people, both at home and in institutions.

The first records of pet-facilitated therapy date from 1792 when rabbits and chickens were introduced into a mental home in York. This was a considerable advance at a time when most mentally ill people were imprisoned and treated callously. Since that time, animals have been used for man's benefit in a variety of ways.

Pets are now used increasingly in institutions. They have been particularly useful in the care of autistic children and in the treatment of a variety of psychiatric disorders. Patients who find it difficult to form relationships with people may find it much easier to form a relationship with an animal. As this relationship develops it can act as a stepping stone towards the formation of relationships with people. Some children's wards keep pets to help create a more homely atmosphere. Many homes for the elderly have periodic visits from pet animals and their owners. The presence of visiting animals often improves relationships between staff and residents and encourages the lonely and withdrawn to participate in conversations, often stimulating happy reminiscences.

In the UK, hospital visiting by dogs is well established. Pro-Dogs is a large charity which runs the PAT dogs scheme (Pro-Dogs Active Therapy). More than 2,500 members visit over 200 institutions on a regular basis. All the dogs used in this scheme have been selected for suitable temperament and freedom from disease.

Working dogs

The role of the guide dog appears obvious: it guides its blind owner and acts as his eyes. In fact a guide dog gives its owner much more than that. The dog greatly improves its handler's mobility and freedom and this enhances the handler's confidence and self esteem. Guide dogs, like pet dogs, also increase the chances of the handler meeting and talking to people.

The relationship that can exist between a working dog and its handler can be extremely close. Most working dogs are highly trained and spend most of their time with the handler both at home and at work. The dog and handler will be together longer than most pet dogs and their owners. In addition to this the handler may rely on his dog for his livelihood and in some cases for his safety.

Most dogs work hard and need to remain very fit. As they grow older their fitness and agility deteriorate and many are retired at a relatively early age, often between 8 and 10 years old.

Frequently, trained working dogs are unable to adapt to retirement and even if the handler keeps the retired dog as a pet, the dog often becomes very jealous when it sees its master taking a new dog to work every day. In such situations, often the only solution is euthanasia. This can be particularly distressing for the handler not only because of the close bonding but there may be a feeling of guilt because the dog is otherwise relatively fit and well.

Summary

The bonds between a pet and its owner are many and varied. Frequently very close attachments are formed between a pet and its owner and it is quite usual and acceptable when the pet dies for the owner to experience a sense of grief proportional to the strength of the attachment.

Chapter 2

Love hurts

I shall walk in the Sun above,
Whose golden light you loved.
I shall sleep alone and, stirring, touch an empty place.
I shall write uninterrupted.
Would that your gentle paw could stir my moving
pen just once again.
I shall see beauty, but none to match
your living grace.
I shall hear music but none so sweet as the
droning song with which you loved me.
I shall fill my days but I shall not, can not, forget.
Sleep soft dear friend, for while I live
you shall not die.

> *Michael Joseph,* Charles – a study of a friendship

Understanding grief

Signs of grief

Factors affecting grief

Stages of grief

Coping with grief

Helping a bereaved pet owner

Comparative grief

Renewed grief

Suppressed grief

Extreme grief and barriers to recovery

Summary

Understanding grief

When a much loved pet dies some people are able to accept the death as the natural conclusion of their pet's life. Others, who have shared only a slight attachment with their pet, can cope quite well with the separation without suffering any real pain. If you have shared a very deep bond with your pet you must expect to experience a deep sense of grief when that animal finally dies.

It is possible to experience a variety of emotions from disbelief, anger, resentment and anguish to a sense of sheer hopelessness. When faced with death you need to express your feelings as much as possible. In order to do this you need an environment that supports your grieving, rather than one that inhibits it. Often it is a lack of understanding about grief, coupled with the insensitivity of those around you, that compounds the misery you feel.

Today British society does not allow people to demonstrate their grief openly; we prefer the bereaved to keep their feelings quietly to themselves – an attitude expressed by C.S. Lewis when he said: 'Perhaps the bereaved ought to be isolated in special colonies like lepers.'

People are often denied the opportunity to discuss their grief because those people that might help and support them are embarrassed by, and unable to understand, the depth of the bereaved pet owner's grief.

You may feel that if you allow yourself to grieve, the grief will take over for ever. The truth of the matter is, if we give ourselves 'permission to grieve', the grief will eventually dissolve. It is only grief that has never been faced that is never resolved.

It is never easy to deal with loss but if you understand a little about what is happening to you, you may find it easier to cope with your bereavement. It is important to:

- Be aware of the stages of grief and typical grief reactions.
- Learn how to cope with your grief.
- Have some idea as to how long grieving may last.
- Be able to recognise the signs of recovery.
- Be aware that some people have problems with grieving.
- Accept that help may be needed with a particularly painful loss.

Signs of grief

When you first learn of the death of your pet you may react by crying and feeling depressed and generally disinterested in life. You may also experience a sense of isolation and anxiety. It is common too, for physical signs to occur.

❏ **Physical signs of grief**

- Loss of appetite
- Fatigue
- Headaches
- Sleeplessness

Persistent thoughts of your dead pet may bother you and you may experience a sense of isolation. It may also be that you feel very angry with your pet for dying and resentful towards other animals just for being alive.

It is normal, healthy and acceptable to grieve over the loss of a pet. It is essential that you face up to the pain of your loss in order to accept it.

Factors affecting grief

The intensity of loss that you may feel is directly related to the strength of the attachment that you felt towards your pet. The more the emotional investment in a relationship, the greater the pain when that relationship is broken. The circumstances surrounding the death and your state of mind at the time also influence the way that you grieve.

Stages of grief

Although there are great differences in the way that people react to grief, in general grieving follows a series of stages, noted below, from initial disbelief to eventual acceptance and recovery.

- Disbelief
- Pain, anger and guilt
- Accepting that your pet will not return
- Channelling your energy into something else

❏ **Disbelief**

The first reaction on hearing of the death of a pet is, inevitably, one of shocked disbelief. Even if the death was expected the reality of death can be very difficult to comprehend. Initially you may experience a sense of numbness which protects you from feeling the full impact of the loss. This numbness may last a few hours or a few days.

People can react very differently at this stage. Someone who was present when her dog was humanely destroyed found that she couldn't leave the dog on its own. She wrapped it in one of her sweaters and placed it in its favourite chair. She spent all evening watching and stroking the dog. It is during this stage of disbelief that you may try to convince yourself that maybe the animal will recover and life will return to normal.

When the death of a pet has been sudden and unexpected the sense of disbelief may last for one or two days and acceptance of the death can be slow to arrive. This point is illustrated in the following case.

One evening a man returned home from work and whilst he was preparing his young cat's favourite meal he let her out for her usual stroll. He heard a commotion outside and went to investigate. He saw his cat on the ground but he wasn't worried because he knew that she often liked to roll around outside. A lady told him that the car hadn't stopped, but he couldn't believe what he was hearing. He rushed the cat to the vet's but it didn't survive. He telephoned his girlfriend to tell her what had happened. 'When she asked if the cat was dead, I found I couldn't use *that* word, I simply said that we didn't have her any more.'

Reluctance to use the words 'dead' and 'death' is common amongst the recently bereaved and it signifies the sense of disbelief that they are experiencing.

The absence of the pet in the house will eventually permeate through to an owner and he will then move on to the next stage of grief.

❏ Pain

This next stage of grief can be the most difficult. It is at this time that you can experience emotions such as anger, guilt, depression and actual pain. This is the time when most pet owners especially need the understanding and support of family and friends.

Anger

When the sensations of disbelief and numbness start to wane you may be overcome by feelings of anger. This anger could be directed at the person apparently responsible for the death, however blameless they may be. The veterinary surgeon who treated your animal can also be a target for your anger.

The need to apportion blame is something that most bereaved pet owners will experience. Sometimes, as illustrated in the next case, we direct our anger at God or fate for allowing our pet to be taken away.

After losing a cat that had shared many happy years with him, an owner bought himself a kitten which was soon tragically killed by a car right outside his house. The owner thought that he had coped well with his first loss but '...felt angry that this time fate or whatever could so casually cut short the life of a delightful little kitten and cause so much sadness.'

This may appear to be a futile kind of anger but it is one that allows you to express your sadness positively.

Guilt

Almost every bereaved pet owner will experience some feelings of guilt following the death of their pet. Rarely is this guilt justified except where negligence or deliberate malice have resulted in the death of an animal. The guilt that may be experienced is similar to the guilt felt in human bereavement.

A common reaction is the one of 'If only... '. On learning of the death of someone it is common to think that *if only* we had not said or done something or *if only* we had done or said something to the deceased person then perhaps we could have prevented the death from occurring.

A case in point concerns the owner who put her dog into kennels whilst she was away on holiday but on her return the flight was delayed by 24 hours. When she went to collect her dog she was told that it had suffered a stroke and died 24 hours earlier. The owner subsequently suffered feelings of guilt and wished that she had never left home; she thought that if she had never gone away the dog would still have been alive. Her guilt was also expressed as anger directed at the airline company because if the plane had been on time she would have been with her dog when it died. With time, emotions like these will fade and it will be possible to accept the fact that nothing could have prevented the pet's death.

Depression

It is possible for bereaved pet owners to suffer from depression following the death of a much loved pet. The owner can feel that they are to blame for the death and they may temporarily feel that life is intolerable without their pet. Feelings of helplessness and hopelessness can affect normal sleeping patterns and cause a lack of appetite. This feeling of depression should not persist and as time passes your interest in life should return. If, for whatever reason, these symptoms persist you should not feel embarrassed to seek help.

Anxiety

It has been reported that bereaved people experience periods of extreme anxiety, often accompanied by episodes of uncontrollable crying. Initially these episodes may be spontaneous and frequent; eventually they will subside and return only with a reminder of the loss.

It is often imagined that the dead pet has returned to a favourite haunt. People may actually 'see' their pet; this tends to happen if a very strong bond existed between a pet and its owner. People also find themselves searching for their dead pet, looking in familiar places and willing them to appear. These reactions can be frightening to the recently bereaved but they are only a natural and expected response of anyone who has recently suffered a major loss.

❏ Acceptance

A further stage of grief occurs once you have accepted the reality of your pet's death. It is essentially the stage when you begin to adjust to an environment in which your pet is no longer a part of your life.

It may be at this time that you dispose of all the reminders of your pet; bowls, leads, toys, collars etc. Some people prefer to put these things away until they can bear to look at them again. One lady kept her cat's collar and would wear it on her wrist whenever she felt in need of the comfort that she once got from her cat.

Photographs can be particularly painful and it may be easier to put these away in a drawer until you can face looking at them again. In contrast to this, some people prefer to display lots of photographs of the dead pet. We all grieve individually and within a family there may be several different ways of coping with the death of a family pet. It is also possible to grieve quite differently over individual pets, because the relationship that you share with one particular pet is quite unique.

❏ Recovery

The final stage of grieving indicates the coming to terms with your loss. It occurs when most of the pain has subsided and you are able to remember your pet with love and affection and recall all the happy times that you shared.

The intensity of the grief that you feel and the length of time it takes you to recover will depend on the type of relationship that you shared with your pet. Other factors such as the age of the pet, for how long you had owned it and the circumstances leading up to and surrounding the death will also influence the duration of your grief.

As an individual you should allow yourself all the time and space you need in which to grieve. It is only by working through your grief that you can finally finish with it.

Replacement

It may be at this point that you start to think about getting another pet. However, for some people the trauma of losing a much loved pet may be too great to risk facing again. These people may make a decision not to own another pet and it is important that this decision is respected by others.

When an animal has captured a very special place in your heart you never really stop missing it; as time progresses you should be prepared for little reminders to bring the occasional lump to your throat.

Coping with grief

After the death of a pet you need to express your feelings; either by talking, if you have a friend who is willing to listen; or perhaps by writing down all your emotions. A lady who lost a dog with whom she had shared a very close attachment was unable to cry or express her grief at the time. One day she sat down and wrote a poem about her dog: '...it acted like a release valve and all my emotions just poured out along with the tears that I'd been unable to shed.'

The main points to remember when you are trying to cope with grief are:

- Give yourself 'permission to grieve'.
- Face the pain as and when it occurs.
- Be aware that you may experience the same stage of grieving more than once and that you may not experience the stages in the order described in this book.
- Allow yourself all the time and space you need to accept your loss. It may take days, weeks or months before you feel that you have recovered from your grief.
- Try and find a way of releasing your emotions; crying, talking or writing may help.
- When you feel that you are nearing recovery be prepared to 'let go' of your dead pet.
- Don't deny yourself the opportunity to love and be loved by another pet if you really feel that you would like one.
- Ensure that other people respect your wishes if you decide, for whatever reason, that you do not want to share your life with another animal.
- Don't be ashamed to seek professional help if you find that you cannot cope with your grief or if your grief has lasted longer than you expected.

Helping a bereaved pet owner

It is understandable that not everyone can comprehend the depth of grief experienced by bereaved pet owners. When confronted by a distressed pet owner it is perhaps better to remain silent and just listen, rather than to pass comments which may appear insincere to the pet owner. The general public can be quite insensitive about pet death and comments like 'It was only a dog' or 'Just go and get another one' are not helpful. They will appear as insulting to the memory of the dead pet and on hearing such remarks people may well withdraw into their own private grief.

The time following pet death can be immensely lonely for the owner. People often rally round and support the bereaved when a human death occurs; but a bereaved pet owner may have no-one with whom to share the grief. The changes in your routine and the feeling of having lost a best friend and perhaps a protector can be particularly painful to bear, especially if your pet was your only close companion.

Although friends and relatives should allow the bereaved pet owner time and space to cope with their loss, the offer of unobtrusive support may be welcomed.

It is often assumed that people can only form deep attachments to sociable animals such as cats and dogs; however, research has shown that it is possible to form relationships with a variety of pets from goldfish through to horses. When an attachment is severed, the pain is no less at the loss of a hamster to which an owner had particular attachment.

It is not only children who develop relationships with small animals such as gerbils, hamsters and rabbits; adults can become equally as fond of them. When the family rabbit died, a middle-aged owner was heard to say: 'I feel such a fool, but I am upset; he was such a part of the family.' The rabbit had assumed the role of 'junior member' of the household since the owner's children had grown up. She felt that she had no real pretext for getting another rabbit and somehow its death had signified the end of an era.

❏ Support

When a member of the community dies it is usual for people to pay their respects to the family of the deceased. This is a courtesy that is rarely extended to bereaved pet owners. It is the reassurance that they have lost something that was immensely important to them that pet owners need and deserve when they are struggling to accept their loss. Nobody can resolve another's grief and it can be difficult to understand the depth of that grief, but to offer some recognition of the loss can be extremely healing for the distraught owner.

❑ Facing the world

After losing your pet you may be so upset that you cannot face going to work or meeting people who may inadvertently ask questions that could add to your distress. Many people force themselves to get on with life and work because they feel that this is what is expected of them. Employers usually don't recognise the trauma which can be caused by the loss of a pet.

If you do find it difficult to continue with work it may be advisable to consult your doctor. This period of deep distress does not usually last longer than a few days.

❑ Dismissal of grief

One reaction that bereaved pet owners are often faced with is dismissal of their grief. People around you may allow you to grieve for a short while but within days they decide that it is time that you returned to normal. Someone who was trying hard to cope but finding that she was 'stuck' in her grief said: 'I am probably pushing all thoughts of my cat to the back of my mind so that I can get on as if nothing had happened, which is what people around me expect me to do.'

The fact that she was suppressing her grief was hindering her eventual recovery.

❑ Solitary grief

There are some pet owners who do not want people to try to help them with their loss. They prefer to grieve alone and work through their feelings quietly in their own way and in their own time. They may occasionally share their feelings with a friend or even a stranger who shows a particular empathy for their loss. It is best to leave these people alone unless they ask for help or fail to recover from their loss.

Comparative grief

There are occasions when the grief you experience on losing a pet is complicated by other emotions which may be linked to your past. One such emotion is guilt, perhaps because you think that you are grieving more for your pet than you did for a parent or relative.

One owner remarked: 'I felt very ashamed to say that I shed more tears on the death of my cat than I did when my mother died.' There is no reason to feel guilty if you react in this way, for the depth of grief experienced is directly related to the relationship shared.

Roles within any human relationship are constantly changing and families often grow apart. In comparison an animal may be with you and dependent on you all its life. It is this constancy and dependency that helps to strengthen the bond between man and his pets. The reason it is possible to feel the loss of a pet so much more acutely than the loss of a parent was summed up by one pet owner: 'I think it must be because I had lived away from home for a long time and rarely saw my parents, but my cats were an essential part of my home.'

Often the differences in the circumstances of death can make one death much more difficult to accept. This is borne out in the following account.

'My mother was 92 and in great pain, the end of her suffering was a welcome release. However my dog was only five years old and full of life. I really couldn't believe it when the vet told me he had cancer. I grieved so much more for my dog – but then I wasn't responsible for the final decision to end my mother's life.'

When the grief suffered by the owner of a dead pet is compared to that felt when a human dies, it is usually the sense of 'loss' that is really being compared. There is no reason to feel ashamed if you feel that you are grieving more for a pet that shared your life on a daily basis than for a parent or relative who has long since ceased to be a part of your everyday existence.

Renewed grief

It has been shown that people often renew the grief they suffered from a previous loss when another death occurs. One pet owner who had lost her husband to whom she had only been married for a short time described her feelings when, three years later, her dog died.

'I can only say, without doubt, the feelings I experienced when my dog died were just as devastating as those I felt when my husband died. Indeed, losing my dog brought back all the pain I had felt when I lost my husband.'

This frequently happens when a pet loss follows the death of a very special person.

It is also possible for a bereaved pet owner to become 'stuck' in grief or to think that the loss has been accepted when suddenly all the anger and guilt return. This is a common reaction amongst the bereaved and people can experience a stage of grieving more than once.

If you experience a feeling of being 'stuck' in your grief then it may be wise to seek counselling help in order to give yourself the opportunity to sit down and talk about your feelings with an experienced listener. It is often by talking to a relative stranger that you begin to realise why you are unable to overcome your grief.

Suppressed grief

When a human dies the feelings of grief and unhappiness are often suppressed. Then, when a pet dies, the grief for the pet is often compounded by the release of these emotions. In one instance a lady became very concerned about her adult son who had seemed to cope well when his father died; although she had thought that he recovered rather quickly. A short time later, the family dog died and her son became very distressed and needed reassurance to help him accept the death of the dog. It appeared that the death of the dog had caused the memories of his father and his unresolved grief to come flooding back. When this happens a person may need help to come to terms with both losses.

Extreme grief and barriers to recovery

Losing a very special pet can affect the physical and mental well-being of the owner. In extreme cases people who prefer the company of animals to that of humans can elevate the status of their pet to that of a human companion. The pet may represent the parent, child, sibling or partner that they have either lost or been denied. This situation is more likely to occur if a person's life lacks emotional fulfilment.

Where a deep bond exists between a pet and its owner the owner may suffer a very deep personal grief when that pet dies. A man who invested a great deal of time and emotion in his relationship with his bitch was totally distraught when she suddenly died whilst walking in the park. He felt that the love he had for his dog was 'a love that most people never experience in a lifetime with a fellow human being.'

After he buried her he said: 'I felt I had also buried my heart.'

When the grief felt by an owner is as extreme as this the person may well become depressed, distant and unable to cope on his own. Anyone experiencing grief as extreme as this should consider seeking professional help to enable them to come to terms with their loss.

Extreme grief can manifest itself as unexplained illness with symptoms which do not necessarily need or respond to medical treatment. These symptoms may appear some time after the loss and at first may not seem to be related to it. In one case a woman was admitted to hospital with unexplained chest pains. After being questioned it was established that she was suffering from stress brought on by the recent death of her dog, by the death of her cat some months earlier and compounded by a car accident in which she had knocked down and killed a stray dog.

Summary

1. Allow yourself to grieve.
2. Face the pain.
3. Realise that grief has no time limit.
4. Accept that grief does not have a set pattern.
5. Find a way to release your feelings.
6. Be prepared to 'let go' of your lost pet.
7. Don't be rushed into making any decisions about a new pet.
8. Be assured that your grief is normal and will, indeed, fade in time.

Chapter 3

A sudden death

Grieve not that I die young. Is it not well
To pass away ere life hath lost its brightness?

Lady Flora Hastings, Swan Song

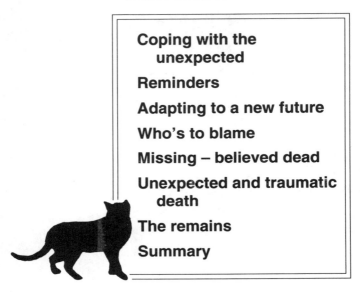

Coping with the unexpected

Reminders

Adapting to a new future

Who's to blame

Missing – believed dead

Unexpected and traumatic death

The remains

Summary

Coping with the unexpected

'I shall never forget that little knock on my front door. My neighbour told me that a cat had been run over, she thought it was mine. I suddenly felt quite ill, my mouth went dry and I started to tremble.'

Many people will be able to sympathise with someone who has had the unenviable task of going out and collecting their dead cat from the road outside their house. The initial reaction of most people to seeing their dead pet is one of shock and disbelief. 'Oh no, not you, I can't believe that it's you.' The suddenness of death can be devastating; it can take several days for the reality of the situation to sink in.

Sudden death inevitably catches owners unawares. Even when an animal is old, we still believe that our pets will be with us for ever.

Many people think that the abruptness of their pet's death is particularly cruel. Initial feelings of shock may be replaced by feelings of anxiety. 'Why me? What have I done to deserve this?'

People begin to search through their lives to find a reason why they have been 'punished' in this way. But they search in vain. There can never be a logical explanation why some animals have their lives cut short so suddenly.

'I have to admit that I believe in fate,' remarked one owner, typically, 'but how could it take such a cruel turn as to take away my Sally?'

The death of a pet can awaken a fear of abandonment in the owner. This fear is more common in children: if a pet can die so suddenly couldn't the child's parents die just as easily and leave the child alone?

Reminders

One of the worst moments following the death of a pet is to return home to a house full of reminders: the food bowl still half full, the lead hanging on its hook by the door, an empty basket. All these things serve as reminders as to the suddenness of events: when the owner left the house everything was normal; in a matter of hours all is shattered.

Many people, unable to face these reminders, will quickly put them away out of sight or throw them away. Others may well be able to draw comfort from having these familiar objects around them. These reminders, although painful at first, are usually a great comfort once the initial pain starts to fade.

Adapting to a new routine

Old habits are difficult to break and owners will find themselves looking for the pet's food bowls at meal times and they will sorely miss the routine of regular walks with their pet. It can take a long time to adjust to a different routine, one which doesn't have to allow for the needs of a pet.

Even familiar walks or meeting people can prove a daunting task for recently bereaved pet owners.

'One of the most difficult things I had to cope with was meeting the other owners who used to exercise their dogs down the same track that I had walked with Jeeves. It must have showed in my eyes because they didn't ask me the one question that I would have found so difficult to answer.'

Who's to blame?

'My husband took our springer spaniel, Ben, for a walk on the common. Once they're on the common my husband usually let Ben off his lead. On this occasion Ben was chased by two other dogs. He ran straight across a busy road and was knocked down and killed instantly by a passing car. The whole family is so shocked and upset. I feel so angry.'

Anger
Anger is an emotion that frequently accompanies the accidental death of a pet. The anger is usually directed at whatever or whoever the owner feels is responsible for the death of their pet. Try to put events into perspective and view the accident as an occurrence for which no-one was really to blame. Trying to accept that accidents do happen can be difficult: but acceptance is an essential part of coming to terms with the sudden death of a pet.

Experiencing the death of a pet in a road accident can make an owner determined that it will never happen again.

'The worst experience I had was when my three-year-old cat was killed just a few yards from my house. Since then I have had my garden completely fenced in. I don't ever want it to happen again.'

Despite precautions like these, cats will still tend to escape and roam and the only answer might be never to let the pet out of the house. In the end most pet owners have to accept that, although they can be extra vigilant, there is no guarantee against a similar accident happening again.

'We did all the wrong things right from the start. We let her out into the garden to climb trees. We lived in the country so we thought it would be safe. She was killed after ten months. It wasn't even a busy road.'

Some owners reproach themselves continually if their pet is killed on the road. They often qualify their feelings of guilt by commenting that they don't live in a busy area. Again, it is important to accept that there is no situation in which you can safely protect a pet 24 hours a day.

'We never let our new cat out of sight. There is no way either of us could cope with the pain again if we lost this cat through something we could have prevented.'

The truth is that animals are as vulnerable as humans and like us they can't avoid the cruel hand of fate.

Self-blame

There are occasions when a death is caused by an omission on the part of the owner.

'I left the back gate open, it leads directly onto the road. My dog got out and I found him dead a few yards up the road.'

Although it was the vehicle that killed the dog, the owner will assume responsibility because the gate was left open. There is no easy way of dealing with this kind of accident. The owner will constantly replay the events in his mind, willing the ending to be different. Unfortunately the facts never change: the dog got out through a gate which the owner had inadvertently left open.

Try to admit openly and honestly to yourself what has happened; accept the fact that your pet was killed accidentally and that constant self-recrimination will do nothing but harm.

Re-experiencing

A sudden death can precipitate a phenomenon known as re-experiencing. Following the shock and trauma of a death, the owner can find himself constantly reliving the events leading up to and surrounding the death. Recurrent dreams may occur and the owner may experience flashbacks of the event coupled with a growing fear of a similar thing happening again. Although re-experiencing may be painful it can be therapeutic too — it is a way of allowing yourself to make some sense out of what has happened.

In some circumstances the owner may have great difficulty re-experiencing one particular part of the event; help may be needed to identify just what it is that is too painful to be faced. In order to come to terms with grief we need to face up to all aspects of it.

When we have re-examined the facts of the death we can sift through them, put them in some sort of order and having done this we can begin to get on with our lives.

Changed perceptions

It is a common misconception that people can revert back to their former selves once they have accepted their loss. The loss of a much loved pet, like the loss of a close human friend or relative, can change your life considerably. You may find that your perception of life and your values of life change once you have worked through your grief.

Missing – believed dead

One of the most difficult aspects of death in a road traffic accident is that the body of the pet may never be found by the owner. The uncertainty caused by a pet's sudden disappearance is a major worry to its owner and it is impossible to grieve for a pet if you're unsure whether it's really dead. Despite the obvious distress caused by seeing their pet dead and possibly disfigured, most pet owners need to see their pet's body to be absolutely sure that it is their pet. Descriptions, no matter how detailed, are unsatisfactory because they still leave room for doubt in the owner's mind.

All dogs over the age of six months are legally required to wear a collar bearing the owner's name and address. There is no legal requirement for a cat to have a collar and identity disc — perhaps if all pets had to have some means of identifying them their owners could be saved a great deal of distress.

❏ Finding an injured animal

If you find an animal lying by the side of the road, or you're unfortunate enough to have knocked one down yourself, there are several things you can do.

If it is safe, stop and check to see if the animal is alive. If it is dead try to move it to the side of the road. Check for any signs of identification. If there are nearby houses ask if anyone recognises the animal.

You are legally required to report any road traffic involving a dog to the police. In any case it is a good idea to inform the police and local veterinary surgeries as they are often asked about missing pets. The police have limited responsibilities towards dogs and none towards cats. This means that it's not really part of their duties to trace lost pets or their owners. In practice this means that some police stations will be more help than others.

A useful thing to do in addition is to put a notice in a local shop or in a local paper.

If the animal is alive but injured you should take steps to get some form of emergency treatment for it. All veterinary surgeons in general practice should provide a 24 hour emergency service for their own clients and to anyone who either doesn't have a regular vet or is unable to go to their own vet.

This doesn't mean that they provide an ambulance service or that they work for free. In most cases they would prefer you to transport the animal directly to their surgery: this saves precious time and the surgery is better equipped to deal with most emergencies.

In the temporary absence of the pet's proper owner you could be responsible for paying for the cost of the emergency treatment. In all cases where an animal is found injured but there is no means of identifying the owner you can contact the RSPCA as they have the power to sanction emergency treatment at their expense.

If you have an accident involving an animal you should endeavour to inform its owner. It is natural to be apprehensive about doing so; we've already said that the owner may feel an initial surge of anger towards the driver of the car. However, most owners are grateful for the information. It may also be in your interest to find the animal's owners as they would be legally liable for any damage caused by their pet, for instance to your car. You, the driver, are not liable for killing the animal nor for the cost of treatment although this is a common misconception.

❏ **Roadside first aid**

1. **Check that the animal is able to breath**. Try to clear any obstructions but don't be tempted to put your hand in its mouth, you may get badly bitten.
2. **Try to reduce serious bleeding** by applying bandages. Don't leave tight bandages on too long, seek urgent veterinary attention.

3. **Move the animal off the road** or verge to some-where safer for both of you. Try to lift the animal carefully in case it has any broken bones. A piece of board or a blanket is very helpful to keep the animal flat.

4. **Try to get the animal to a veterinary surgery** as soon as possible. It is vital to ring the surgery before you set out to make sure that someone is there when you arrive. Tell them if it's not your animal.

5. **Always ensure your own safety**. Muzzle the animal to avoid being bitten especially if the animal is in great pain. In the case of dogs, a bandage or thick cord can be used to bind the animal's mouth shut.

6. **Prevent dogs from running away** or back onto the road by putting them on a lead.

7. **Keep the animal warm and don't give it any-thing to eat or drink** until it has been seen by a vet.

Remember also to:

- check for any means of identification;
- inform the local police and
- try to inform the animal's owner.

Unexpected and traumatic death

❏ Saying goodbye

'Cindy was only 16 months old, she was very lively with a glossy coat and bright eyes. She suddenly started to vomit continuously. The vet performed some tests but was unable to find out what was wrong. The vomiting continued so I agreed to let the vet carry out an exploratory operation.'

This is a common story of how a healthy young pet suddenly becomes ill. This particular owner left her cat overnight at the vet's with the instructions that if the operation revealed an incurable problem, the cat should not be allowed to regain consciousness. Despite her decision, it was still a shock when the vet rang the next day with the bad news. The operation had shown that the cat had an inoperable cancer and that she only had a few weeks to live. The owner couldn't sentence her young pet to a lingering death and confirmed that she didn't want the cat to be allowed to wake up. Afterwards she found great difficulty accepting the death of her pet.

'It is so hard to come to terms with her death, she was so fit one minute and gone the next. She was only a normal tabby, not even pretty, but she was mine.'

It wasn't just the fact that death was so sudden that made it so difficult to accept; in addition the owner had never said goodbye as she thought her pet would only be kept in overnight.

Pet owners can suffer dreadfully if they are denied the opportunity to hold their pet for one last time and say goodbye. Saying goodbye is such an important part of accepting death as a reality that if this important symbolic act is denied an owner then it may be comforting to hold a simple ceremony in memory of the pet. This could be the burial of the pet or planting something in its memory.

❏ Feelings of guilt

Occasionally a pet dies as a result of a game going horribly wrong. After taking her dog for its usual morning walk an owner was playing with it in her back garden. The dog's favourite game was fetching the tennis ball that her owner would throw for it. On that morning the dog swallowed a piece of the ball and choked to death in front of its owner.

The first few days were taken up by the horror of how she had died. 'I wept when I went past the familiar walks: the pain was worse in the evenings when I had no dog to sit by my feet when I returned home from work.'

When an animal dies like this an owner is bound to experience a sense of guilt; 'If only I hadn't been playing with her, if only I hadn't bought that ball,' the list can be endless. It doesn't matter how many 'ifs' there are, the fact remains that the dog died accidentally doing something that it loved to do, playing ball with its owner.

The owner couldn't save her pet but at least she was present at its death, she eventually gained some degree of solace from knowing she was there to comfort it at the end.

In these sad circumstances, the shock and horror of the death may stay with the owner for some time and similar situations may cause extreme anxiety.

❏ Anger

Sometimes pets are attacked and killed by other animals. 'Our cat Angus was in our front garden, he wasn't afraid of dogs and when two dogs ran over to him he didn't run away. The dogs just picked him up and shook him. I think they must have broken his neck because there wasn't a mark on him.'

This owner wasn't there to witness the attack herself, but she was told by a neighbour when she returned home. 'We all felt so guilty for not being there at the time to protect him. We also felt guilty and angry that he wasn't safe even in his own garden.'

When an animal dies in this way anger frequently surfaces: anger at the unnecessary loss of life and anger because the death could have been prevented if other pet owners kept their pets under proper control.

It is extremely traumatic to actually see your pet killed in this way. Sebbie was a small Yorkshire terrier who in a relatively short space of time had become extremely attached to his master. He went everywhere with him sometimes sitting in the basket on his master's bicycle, sometimes trotting along behind. On this particular day Sebbie was running along behind his master on a usually deserted towpath. Ahead was a moored barge and the two occupants were picnicking on the bank of the canal. Sebbie's owner also noticed two large dogs running off the lead but he didn't anticipate any danger.

Suddenly one of the dogs rushed up, grabbed Sebbie and shook him violently by the neck. Sebbie's owner could hardly believe what was happening but he managed to pull him free. Sebbie died on the way to the vet's. The owner of the dog offered to pay for Sebbie to be cremated but this was no recompense for a man who had just lost a true friend.

'I have felt really ill and depressed since it happened. The memory of seeing him killed in such a brutal fashion will remain as a scar for the rest of my life.'

Some owners may find it helpful to consider the other side of the coin, namely the guilt suffered by responsible pet owners who have to acknowledge that their pet was responsible for the death of another animal. One woman was so distraught when her dog attacked a sheep whilst they were out walking in the country that she seriously considered having the dog humanely destroyed.

The pet's remains

A sudden death may well pose the previously unconsidered question of what should be done with the pet's remains. Often in this situation owners will be too distressed to make a reasoned decision and may make one that they might later regret. This a question that all pet owners should consider from time to time because no matter what the circumstances, death, when it comes, is always an unexpected shock.

Summary

1. The sudden death of a pet is accompanied by a feeling of disbelief that can last for hours or days.
2. Be prepared to feel angry that your pet has died so suddenly, perhaps by means beyond your control.
3. If you were partly to blame for your pet's death, try to accept your guilt, because this is the best way to overcome it.
4. Recognise that the sudden death of a pet may change your life considerably.
5. If you find an injured or dead domestic pet, try to inform its owners – uncertainty is worse then knowing the truth.
6. If your pet dies suddenly try to see it one more time, to say goodbye. Saying goodbye is an important step towards accepting the reality of the pet's death.

Chapter 4

What to tell the children

A simple child,
That lightly draws its breath,
And feels its life in every limb,
What should it know of death?
                    William Wordsworth, We are Seven

Children and pets

Helping children cope with losing a pet

Symptoms of grief in children

The family and pet loss

Euthanasia

Burial and funerals

Some practical points

A section for children to read themselves

Summary

Children and pets

'Over the two very short years that I had with him, Paddy taught me more than any one person had ever done. We went everywhere together, we laughed and cried together, we understood each other.'

Like adults, children and adolescents can form deep relationships with companion animals. Children today grow up in a rapidly changing world, life has changed so much that our children are totally unlike we were at their age, their fears and needs are different from ours. Modern families are smaller and less likely to live in the same place for long; in this environment a pet can fill the role of a substitute friend or relative.

Children generally find it easy to form relationships with pets. The depth of these relationships is often not fully appreciated by parents and other adults. If parents can understand what the pet meant to the child they may be able to help the child cope with its loss.

Children become attached to a variety of pets from gerbils to horses. When their interest in horses is stimulated at an early age, it can remain with them throughout life.

Children are usually taught to ride in a 'school' atmosphere, where certain behaviour standards are demanded of them. It is, perhaps, due to this that a feeling of respect for horses is developed by the young rider.

Animals that can return affection are perhaps more likely to stimulate this response than the very small animals. However, the relationship that develops between any child and its pet is unique to them, and should be treated with equal importance, irrespective of the species involved.

The death of a pet is often the child's first encounter with death. If it is handled sensitively and honestly, the child may learn a lot about love, life and loss. This knowledge can help the child to cope with future bereavements.

Helping children cope with losing a pet

In order to help a child with pet loss there are three factors to consider:

- What the pet actually meant to the child.
- The child's understanding of death.
- The way in which the actual death is handled.

❏ The pet's role

The role of a pet in a child's life alters as the child grows older and more independent.

Birth-1 year

Infants less than six months old need little more than physical comfort and a well trained pet can help fill the gap when an infant's parents are unable to pick it up and cuddle it. Infants over six months start to recognise individuals — especially their mother. A familiar pet can provide emotional support as well as physical comfort if the child's parents are not continually present; this reduces the child's anxiety and increases its trust in its environment.

1-2 years

Between the ages of 1 and 2 years, playing with a family pet stimulates crawling and walking, and encourages independence and activity. The pet acts as a protector as the child begins to explore its world.

It is also at this age that children learn to say the word 'no'; this naturally leads to battles of will with parents. At times like these a child needs a non-judgmental friend and protector that doesn't criticise. Equally important the child can see that, although the pet is scolded, it is still loved. This reassures the child of a parent's love despite a scolding.

It is easy for a child to believe that being naughty can lead to illness: 'don't do that,' a parent might say, 'or you'll make yourself sick.' The presence of a pet that doesn't get ill when it misbehaves or becomes ill for no apparent reason, shows that this is not necessarily so. The presence of a pet can also act as an incentive for a child to convalesce rapidly after an illness.

2-6 years

Children between 2 and 6 years develop their imaginations and indulge in 'magical' thinking; in the world of their imagination wishes come true. In real life they can wish their pet away but the fact that nothing happens helps the child to realise that hostile thoughts don't become deeds or cause physical harm.

A pet can fill the role of a playmate or sibling; this is especially important in the case of an only child. The pet is often included in the child's daydreams and is imagined to have all sorts of qualities and abilities. In the absence of a pet or a playmate, a child will usually invent an imaginary one. A real pet can guide a child away from his imaginary inner world towards the real world outside.

As the child becomes older it can be entrusted with increasing responsibility for the care of a pet and this helps to develop the child's sense of self esteem. Responsibility also helps the child learn that a pet is not a toy that can be put away and forgotten; that it needs love and care every day.

Children have to make the transition from playing alone to playing with friends. This can be a traumatic process that causes a great deal of anxiety and insecurity. In this respect, a pet can help a child in two ways: firstly, by providing the love and acceptance that the child needs if it is feeling vulnerable or if its advances towards other children are rebuffed; secondly, pets also make a positive contribution towards the child making friends. They can attract other children, can help to break the conversational 'ice' and improve a child's status in the eyes of friends.

6-12 years

From the age of six years children become more and more independent of their parents and so the presence of a pet as a protector both at home and outdoors is a great comfort.

It is from the age of six that children become aware of their sexual identity, the presence of a pet is a natural way for children to gain experience of sexual behaviour.

Children of this age group can assume increasing responsibility for the care of their pet; this may involve the acquisition of certain skills or knowledge. Training a pet helps to show that learning a skill takes time and effort. Some children will also learn that sometimes sacrifices have to be made to help others, especially if the pet becomes ill and needs expensive treatment or constant nursing.

Children can learn about other people by observing how they treat animals, kindly or cruelly. Children in their early teens often start to show an interest in protecting the environment and preventing cruelty to animals.

Children entering adolescence often feel the need to distance themselves from their parents, boys in particular feel embarrassed about showing their emotions. A pet can provide the comfort and support that an adolescent needs when things go wrong but is too embarrassed to seek help from parents or friends.

After a bad day at school or an argument with parents, a pet can seem to be the only companion not being critical. You can tell a pet all your worries and secrets and it won't tell a soul!

❏ Conception of death

The way a child perceives death will depend on age, personality, emotional development and the nature of the attachment between the child and the pet.

Birth-5 years

Children under five years of age don't perceive death as permanent but as a form of temporary separation. This is a view reinforced by children's cartoons in which characters are frequently blown to bits only to return unharmed. Children in this age group believe that death can be avoided by being good or careful. They are distressed by the physical separation from their pet and the fact that they wrongly view the separation as temporary doesn't make their distress any less real.

Four weeks after getting a Siamese kitten, a little girl of two-and-a-half years was extremely upset when it died quite unexpectedly. Along with her four-year-old brother, she was allowed to see the dead body and say goodbye to it. Typical of her age, she had difficulty accepting what 'dead' meant and for many weeks after the death she told everyone she met that Ming had gone away. At first she added: 'He's coming back,' but after repeated explanations by her mother, she replaced this with: 'One day a new kitten will come.'

The two children began to play games where either one of them, or a toy, was dead. The child would lie still on the floor and watch people's reactions. The little boy would tell his sister to cry, because this is what you did when something died. He had no difficulty in accepting that Ming would not return. Some 18 months previously he had been allowed to watch as the family cat was buried in the garden and he knew that as that cat had not returned, there was no reason to expect that Ming would. After the little girl was given a toy rabbit, which she decided to call Ming, talk of the kitten began to fade and her affections were transferred to the toy.

Despite not talking much about their feelings, even children in this age group can react deeply to pet loss.

Even after three months a mother found her three-year-old son, stroking a photograph of his cat whilst sobbing. She said he had regularly cried at night and had nightmares about the accident.

Children this age need a lot of support and reassurance that they are safe and that their parents or guardian are not about to die and abandon them.

5-9 years

Between their fifth and ninth years, children begin to realise that death *is* final, inevitable and universal. This realization is often accompanied by a desire to believe in an afterlife. Children of this age often view death as a personality such as The Grim Reaper, who can be avoided by being lucky or clever.

Because children in this age group are able to comprehend the meaning of death, they can benefit from talking about their pet, its illness and death, and their feelings of loss. They need to feel that other people, especially adults, realise how important their pet was to them. It is vital that parents do not try to pretend that nothing happened or that the pet never existed, because their children will regard this as an attempt to devalue their pet and their grief at its death.

'It didn't matter that my kitten was dead. I learned from experience that adults didn't care if your pet was killed.'

9-12 years

From the age of nine, children realise that separation and loss can affect them. Many children experience fears of abandonment either through death or divorce.

Children of this age are generally considered old enough to take on the responsibility of caring for a healthy animal, and they are also old enough to be involved in the care of their pet when it becomes ill. These children are quite able to express their feelings about pets and pet loss, and they should be encouraged to talk or write about their feelings rather than keep them bottled up.

They are aware of death and they can usually accept the inevitability of death through old age quite readily. Equally they can show anger and guilt when a pet dies. Children of this age are also able to look forward in time and envisage their probable feelings of grief when their pet eventually dies, often saying things such as: 'He's my best friend, and I just don't know what I'd do without him.'

Teenagers

Most teenagers have an adult concept of death and are just as capable of grieving for their pets as their parents.

The following is an account by a 15-year-old girl of the terminal illness of the aged family cat.

'Tommy had to be put to sleep to relieve him of the pain. Even though "putting him down" was the kindest thing to do, we still felt sad. We cried a lot. Tommy's death was just like a family death and I suppose that is exactly what it was.'

Unfortunately, sometimes the adult emotions displayed by teenagers are coupled with great embarrassment at showing their grief. Children of this age need proper explanations and the opportunity to take part in any decision making about their pet.

Symptoms of grief in children

Children may appear to cope very well with the loss of a pet but it may be several weeks later that parents and teachers notice changes in a child's sleep or behaviour patterns.

Common symptoms of grief in children

- Initial disbelief and denial of the death.
- Crying, anger, guilt and depression.
- Loss of toilet training in young children.
- Nightmares and unnecessary worry about small hurts.
- Complaints of subjective illnesses, e.g. headaches and stomach aches, by older children.
- Greatly increased anxiety when separated from parents or other familiar carers.
- Anger towards siblings and playmates, and even towards parents and the vet for not preventing the pet's death.

❏ Handling feelings of guilt

When a pet dies many children suffer feelings of guilt. Such feelings can also be experienced when a family pet has to be rehomed for some reason.

43

Months after the family dog was rehomed, a teenage girl was still showing extreme signs of distress. She had been responsible for its care and exercise, and although her mother explained that she had feared the dog might show hostility towards the baby she was about to have, the girl simply could not accept what had happened. She, in fact, assumed that it was her fault that the dog had to go as she was responsible for the welfare of the pet.

Situations like this need very careful handling. Clear explanations and reassurance of why the pet has had to be rehomed should be given to any children in the family home.

Young children who have wished that the pet would go away may feel that this has led to its disappearance. Older children may feel guilty if a personal lapse, such as leaving a gate open, contributed to a pet's death.

❏ Coping with anger

Children are just as likely to experience anger when a pet dies as their parents.

When a 13-year-old returned from school to discover that her pet rabbits had been savaged and killed by a dog, her immediate response was one of extreme anger. 'I went into the dining room and sat in my favourite chair. I punched the sides of that chair until my knuckles were red. I swore that I would never stroke another dog.' Having released her emotions, this girl found that her hostility towards dogs faded as she eventually accepted that what had happened was a dreadful accident.

In addition a child may blame its parents for not doing enough to save the pet. Children are not aware that some diseases are incurable, that quality of life may be more important than quantity, and that sometimes treatment is just too expensive to continue.

The family and pet loss

The whole family can be affected by the loss of a child's pet. If the family accept the death as a 'common' loss and they grieve together for that loss, this will encourage the child to show its feelings too. Sharing feelings will greatly lessen the burden of the individual child. A child needs to be reassured that it is normal to grieve for any loss of life.

WHAT TO TELL THE CHILDREN

If parents take pet loss seriously, children will learn that it does matter when a pet dies. In addition they will learn to show respect for other people's feelings.

When a family pet dies it is all too easy for parents to be so grief stricken themselves that they forget that their children might be just as distressed and need help and support.

❏ Telling the truth

A child should always be told the truth about pet loss and death. Parents are often tempted to tell 'white' lies about the death of a pet in order to shield their children from distress. In fact parents tend to under-estimate their children's ability to cope with bad news. Children usually find the truth acceptable; it is fabrications that they find confusing and difficult to understand. If a pet is killed on the road it is extremely unwise to tell a child it ran away and became lost, not least because the child will expect it to return one day.

As one child said, subsequently: 'I wish I had known the truth because I would have accepted it instead of worrying about the fate of my pet and constantly looking for it.'

Wherever possible children should be included when making decisions about a pet's welfare.

❏ A missing pet

When a pet goes missing it is important to be as realistic as possible. Don't give the child too much hope that the pet will reappear in a few days. Explain that you don't know what has happened to the pet but that you are doing everything you can to find out. Encourage the child to participate in searching, making enquiries and putting up notices.

If, after a few weeks, there is still no trace of your pet it is important to hold some kind of ceremony to honour the memory of the pet. This will allow the child to "say goodbye" to the pet and to begin to grieve for it. If children see that the whole family is accepting the situation then they will as well. Too many children have suffered from waiting at the garden gate for their pet to return because they have either not been told the truth or not been able to accept the reality of the situation.

Euthanasia

It is wise to warn children if a family pet is likely to die or to be helped to die painlessly in the near future.

Young children

Children less than six years old have little conception of the meaning of death, therefore they need emotional support rather than details. It is important to emphasise that the pet is dying because it is very sick and that it is being helped to die more easily. Explain very clearly there is a difference between the pet's illness and the child's minor childhood ailments. Try to avoid using the phrase 'put to sleep', because this can cause sleeping problems or a fear of general anaesthesia.

Older children

Older children need more detailed, age-appropriate descriptions and honest answers to their questions. Children who have cared for the well pet should be given the chance to nurse and comfort their pet until the time comes for euthanasia. A child that is old enough to nurse an ill pet deserves to be told exactly what euthanasia involves. Equipped with this knowledge your child can decide for itself whether to be present or not.

One 14-year-old girl made the conscious decision to be present when Ari, her toy poodle who was extremely ill with diabetes, died.

'I held him while the vet inserted the needle and I felt him get heavier in my arms and I knew that he was no longer with us.'

The fact that she had been present whilst euthanasia was carried out, seemed to help her accept the reality of what had happened: 'I cuddled him, wishing that he was alive and well, but I knew I could not turn back the clock and that life had to carry on.'

If the life of a pet is to be ended it is important to let your children know that it is about to take place; failure to do this deprives the children of the chance to say goodbye to the pet.

'I thought I had prepared my three children for the impending death of their dog but I hadn't. My husband and I could not bear to watch our children say goodbye to the dog so we took it to the vet whilst the children were at school. I have never forgiven myself for this. I felt I let them down badly and deprived them of facing up to the reality of what had happened.'

WHAT TO TELL THE CHILDREN

If the children are not present at the time of death, parents should consider letting them see the dead pet's body. This helps children realise that the pet is dead, to start to grieve for the loss and ultimately to come to terms with it.

It is important to allow older children, especially adolescents, to have some say in the decision to end the family pet's life; otherwise, once the pet is dead, parents may find themselves the focus of their children's anger. Anger is a normal reaction to grief and in addition children may feel angry that their parents made the decision alone and that in their opinion they made the wrong decision, or that the decision was made too soon. Parents must be prepared for this; it isn't advisable to divert the anger by blaming the vet or other people.

Children and the euthanasia of the family pet

Do
- Inform the children of the pet's impending death.
- Answer questions honestly, and be prepared to answer the same question again and again.
- Let children be present if they want to be.
- Allow children to say goodbye.
- Emphasise the difference between the pet's serious illness and the child's minor ailments.
- Allow children to have a role in making the decision.
- Let the child know that it's normal, healthy and acceptable to grieve for the loss of a pet.
- Have a 'funeral'.
- Talk about the dead pet.

Don't
- Force children to be present.
- Have a pet's life ended without telling the children.
- Say the pet ran away because the children will hope for it to come back.
- Use the euphemism 'put to sleep' as this might produce phobias about sleep or anaesthesia.
- Blame the vet. Admit *you* made the decision.
- Feel you have to hide your emotions, your children will be relieved to see that you're upset too.
- Have euthanasia carried out on a birthday or holiday, because that will act as an annual reminder of the pet's death.

Burial and funerals

Burials and funerals are usually very important as far as children are concerned. Burying a pet's remains as a family is another way of showing children that they aren't the only family members to be distressed. It is another way of helping children to accept that the pet is dead and can never return and provides the chance for them to say goodbye to the pet.

Even if there is no body to bury, either because the pet was cremated or the pet has disappeared, a small memorial service can help the child accept that the pet has gone for good.

Attendance at a pet's burial should be entirely optional, no one should be forced to attend.

Children are very concerned that their pet's remains should be treated with dignity and burial at home helps to reassure them that this is so.

Children like to arrange 'funerals' for their pets themselves. In Bristol a group of friends who shared a common love of small pets would hold a ceremony at the bottom of the pet's garden. On one such occasion, a small hamster was being placed in the ground, sombre music was flowing out of the lounge window and all the children were saying their goodbyes, when a light aircraft flew overhead. The youngest member of the group stared up at the plane and asked 'Has Jesus come to collect him already?'

Whatever parents decide to tell their children about death is entirely up to them, and is usually based on their own religious beliefs. However, young children often accept the explanation that the pet has gone to play in God's garden.

It is a good idea to erect a small memorial or plant a tree or bush in the pet's memory. This serves as a reminder to a young child that the pet will not return.

Some practical points

❏ Common reactions to pet loss

- Common repetition of questions: 'Where is the pet?', 'Is he coming back?', Was he ill?'.
- Anxiety over the welfare of other family pets: 'Will our dog die too?'
- Concern that a new pet may also die.
- Repeated requests to see the grave of the pet.
- Questions about where the dead pet goes.
- Games in which the child or their toys are dead.

❏ Misconceptions

Children can become confused about death because of the terminology used by family and friends.

The commonest misconception is formed when the euphemism 'put to sleep' is used. The child can think either that if the pet is asleep, then surely it will awaken; or that if the pet does not awaken from its sleep, that the child itself too is in danger of not awakening from sleep.

Telling a child that the pet *goes* to heaven when it dies can also be misleading, as the parents of one young child discovered. The little girl became very distressed because her cat had been run over and somebody had moved the body. The child assumed that as there was no body, the cat couldn't go to heaven.

When dealing with young children, it is advisable to use very simple explanations, choosing words carefully.

❏ A simple explanation of death

- Your pet has died.
- This means that it no longer moves or breathes.
- We will bury the body.
- You can visit the grave and talk about it whenever you want to.
- We are all very sad and we should cry whenever we need to.

❏ Souvenirs and reminders

When a pet dies children tend to keep their feelings to themselves, perhaps feeling embarrassed to express them. One way in which parents can help children to cope is to encourage them to write about their pet or perhaps to create a scrap book containing photographs of the pet. Writing about the pet can be very therapeutic even if the child doesn't want anyone else to read what has been written.

❏ Replacement

Children are like adults: most of them benefit from time to grieve for one pet before they find another one to take its place. If parents supply a child with a new pet immediately after the death of the old one they are, in effect, telling the child that pets are unimportant because they are so easily replaced and therefore that the child's grief is unnecessary.

It is a good idea to ask children if and when they would like a replacement. One 11-year-old girl recalled that when she was five her pet hamster had died and she subsequently suffered repeated nightmares about the loss. It was because of this that her parents would not allow her another pet for six years. When she eventually got a pet rabbit she became very attached to it and said that if she had been allowed another hamster when she was five, it would have helped her cope with her loss.

It would seem that the best solution to the difficult problem of replacement is to discuss it with the child and address their personal needs and wishes.

If a child seems particularly attached to a pet, it may be worth acquiring another pet before the old one dies. In this way the child has a chance to become attached to the new pet and it also gives the child some comfort when the older pet does die.

A section for children to read themselves.

- A pet can be a very important part of your life. A pet can be like a friend and you can take care of it as well as play with it.
- It can sometimes be difficult to care for a pet: they are not like toys. They have the same needs as you do for food, drink, love, attention, exercise and treatment when they are ill.
- Animals do get ill occasionally, just like you do. When an animal is sick you take it to a vet.
- Vets will sometimes do tests on your pet, like blood tests or X-rays, to find out what is wrong. Some pet illnesses can be treated but some cannot.
- When an animal gets very old, or very ill, or gets very badly injured in an accident, the vet may advise you that the kindest thing to do for your pet is to allow it to die peacefully rather than let it suffer.
- You may feel very sad when your pet dies and the hurt can last for a while. It does help if you talk about your feelings and you allow yourself to cry and be sad. The pain will go away and you will then have all the happy memories of your pet. It will only keep hurting if you try to ignore your feelings of sadness.
- It can be difficult to understand what 'dead' means; but essentially it means that the animal has stopped breathing and moving. Once an animal is dead it can never come alive again.
- When people talk about 'putting an animal to sleep' they do not really mean that the animal is asleep, they mean that the animal has been helped to die by the vet, to save it suffering pain unnecessarily. You know that when you go to sleep at night, you will wake up again in the morning, but when an animal or person is dead they will never wake up again.
- You may miss your pet a lot and feel lonely and sad. It is normal to feel like this and most people who lose a pet feel the same way. People don't always show how upset they are because they think that other people won't understand them.

WHAT TO TELL THE CHILDREN

- It can seem unfair and such a waste of life when pets die especially if they are young and their death is unexpected. You may feel angry at what has happened. Try to talk to someone about your anger.

- People often feel guilty when their pet dies, especially if they think that they had not been very nice to it or had wished the pet was not around any longer. Some people feel that it is their fault that the pet died, but in most cases no one is to blame. It is normal to feel responsible in some way.

- You might find yourself wishing that you could have done something to stop your pet from dying or wish you could make your pet come alive again.

- When a pet dies, you and your family have to decide what to do with its body. The vet may arrange for the remains to be cremated or you may want to take your pet home and bury it in the garden.

- People often bury their pets in places where the pet liked to be. You can mark the grave with a headstone or plant a bush or tree in your pet's memory.

- If you bury your pet it is helpful for all the family to be there to help support each other in their sadness.

- You will probably find that you need to spend some time alone to think about your dead pet.

- You may like to keep a photograph of your pet to remember it by. People often keep other reminders like collars or a favourite toy.

- When you start to feel better, you may begin to think about getting another pet. You will know when you are ready and you shouldn't be rushed into making a decision.

- Losing your pet will teach you a lot about life. You will start to realise that it is normal to feel sad when you lose something you love.

- In time you will find that allowing yourself to feel sad will help you to recover from your loss and eventually you will start to feel better.

Summary

1. Children form deep attachments to pets and they can be very upset when a pet dies.
2. Pets have different roles to play as children grow up.
3. A child's understanding of death changes as it becomes older.
4. A child may not show obvious signs of grief immediately.
5. Try to grieve as a family and do not dismiss your child's grief.
6. Talk to the child in simple but truthful terms about what has happened to the pet.
7. Reassure the child of the normality of their feelings.
8. Children need to know that their pet's body has been treated with respect; burials and memorials can help to confirm this.
9. Include the child in major decisions about the pet.
10. Be guided by the child whether to get another pet and if so, when.

Chapter 5

Pets and the elderly

Tears, idle tears, I know not what they mean,
Tears from the depth of some divine despair
Rise in the heart, and gather to the eyes,
In looking on the happy Autumn-fields,
And thinking of the days that are no more.

Alfred, Lord Tennyson, The Princess

Benefits of pet ownership

Pet loss

Replacement

A case history

Benefits of pet ownership

Pet ownership is known to improve health, and this is equally true for people of all ages. In today's society families often live miles apart and so a pet may become the only 'family' that an elderly person sees regularly. A pet may become the focal point of an older person's life, indeed a pet can become his or her reason to live.

❑ A link with the past

A pet can provide a valuable link with a deceased spouse or relative, offering comfort to the owner because they too once shared the pleasure of the deceased's company. It is the shared memories that can make the pet so special. Many bereaved people draw comfort from the hope that the pet will accompany them into old age and so, when the pet dies it may be that the last living link with a deceased spouse or close friend has been removed, greatly intensifying the grief for the pet by renewing grief for the deceased person.

A pet is not only a reminder of absent friends it is also a reminder of happy times, events and places. When a pet dies it is the end of an era in our lives.

'Ben wasn't really my dog, he was my husband's. We bought him when Eric, my husband, retired. I've had to look after him since Eric died in 1986 and now losing Ben is like losing Eric again.'

❏ Motivation

On a practical level a pet can give an owner motivation; to get up in the morning, to keep warm, to take exercise and to eat regularly. People living on their own often feel that it is too much of an effort to feed themselves properly but when they have the needs of a pet to consider they may well take more of an interest in shopping, food and in life in general.

❏ Independence

As people become older they find that their independence diminishes; looking after a pet can be an important morale booster for an elderly person who may be reliant on other people for nearly everything else.

❏ Exercise

A pet can provide an older person with a reason to take exercise, something he may be reluctant to take on his own. Taking a dog for walks several times a day gives an owner the opportunity to go outdoors into the fresh air.

❏ Companionship

One of the most important elements of pet ownership for the older person must surely be the companionship, love and loyalty that a pet provides, often at a time when friends may be getting scarce and relatives too far away or too busy to keep in regular contact. For some people their pet may be their sole companion and confidante, thus representing an important part of their everyday life.

❏ Meeting people

Keeping a pet can provide a valuable social link between an owner and the outside world. Research shows that people taking pets for a walk are much more likely to speak to somebody than people without pets, perhaps because they are perceived to be more 'safe', perhaps because the pet acts as a social lubricant; people can pat it, admire it and talk about it. Even short chats can be very welcome to older people who face the prospect of returning to an empty home; talking to a passerby may be the only human conversation they'll have all day.

Even if an elderly pet owner is unable to take their pet for a walk personally, they will probably have a younger dog walker who helps them. Talking to the walker helps to break the loneliness and monotony of being confined indoors largely on one's own. Dog walkers can also help in other ways: they can keep an eye on both dog and owner and they can often help with other small but vital errands.

Even trips to the vet's surgery bring the owner into contact with other people and, because the animals provide a conversation topic, vets' waiting rooms are usually more sociable than doctors'.

❏ Security

An animal living with an older person, especially one who lives alone, provides a sense of security in a very uncertain world. A dog barking is a very effective deterrent against strangers. Even cats with their sensitive sight and hearing can help an owner by warning of danger that the owner hasn't detected.

❏ A mutual interest

Animals are not just important to older people who live alone, they can be just as important to elderly people living together. A pet can provide a shared interest for two people and become a precious family member to nurture and gain pleasure from.

Many people acquire a pet to share their retirement; after a lifetime of work it can be difficult coping with idleness and being together all day long, a pet can provide a common interest and a perpetual topic of conversation.

Pet loss

For elderly people, especially those who live alone or are house-bound, the companionship that a pet can bring is inestimable and the loss of that pet can be devastating, as one grandmother noted.

PETS AND THE ELDERLY

'When Sam passed away last December his loss was devastating. I am partially disabled and somewhat housebound, so I relied on him so much. His loss has left such an awful vacuum.'

The death of a much loved pet can leave the owner feeling that his or her purpose for living has also died. This can even lead to thoughts of suicide.

'Perhaps I grieved so much because we were so close and such good friends. It was just plain old fashioned love on both sides. She was my stand-by, my comforter and my consolation during a very unhappy period in my life. When she died I felt totally abandoned. I even felt suicidal as everything seemed to have been taken away from me and I was left with nothing.'

It is not only the sense of abandonment that can distress an elderly person but also the fact that the death of a pet serves as a painful reminder that death is the ultimate fate of us all. A death always makes us review our lives and the death of a close companion makes us even more aware of our own mortality.

For some people the death of a pet is significant because they know that this pet is the last one they will ever own because they are now too old to start again.

Although the death of a pet can be very disturbing for the older pet owner most people would not have missed the companionship of their pet for anything.

'The loss of Sacha was a great shock to me. I am 69 years old and she was more to me than just a lovely pet, more like a child, a totally integrated member of the family. I would not have believed the pain of her sudden departure. But I am so glad to have owned her, for without her, life would have been purposeless.'

One of the difficult aspects of any pet owner's grief is having to return home to an empty house every day.

'For many days afterwards I felt mentally, emotionally and physically shattered. I am only now beginning to come to terms with the situation. My cat was my sole companion for more than 10 years. Now, at the age of 65, I find myself having to adjust to the situation when for the first time in my life I am the only living person in the house. It is like having to adjust to retirement all over again; when I retired nine years ago my whole life became geared towards caring for my pet.

'I am fortunate that I have so many outside interests, but inevitably there are occasions when I am alone and it is at these moments that the loss is felt most deeply. Surprisingly I have found that the lack of responsibility almost brings forth a feeling of guilt in that I no longer have to consider the needs of another being.'

Replacement

Life can be very difficult when you have spent the last ten years focusing your life on your pet – it can seem very empty and meaningless. One of the problems faced by the older pet owner is whether or not to get another pet. This is a problem for all pet owners and is dealt with elsewhere. There are, however, additional aspects to the decision-making process for older pet owners to consider.

When a pet dies, many pet owners wait for a while before they find a replacement, partly to get over their grief and partly to enjoy their new found freedom. After a lifetime spent raising children and looking after pets, some people are ready for a change, a chance to go away for weekends or on long foreign holidays.

No decision is irreversible. Lots of people find that after a few months of 'freedom' they start to miss owning a pet: no walks, no companionship, no mess! Ultimately many people change their minds and acquire a new pet.

It is important to realise that the person looking for a new pet is probably 10 to 15 years older than when its predecessor was acquired. This must influence the choice of species and breed.

Despite the fact that owning a pet is beneficial, especially to someone who is ill or in some way disabled, many older people are prevented from enjoying the benefits of pet ownership because they are too ill or too frail to look after a pet on their own. Pet ownership must not be undertaken if the animal's welfare cannot be *fully* ensured.

❏ Choosing a suitable pet

Species

A partial answer to the problems outlined above is to think carefully about the type of pet that you choose and what you need your pet for. A dog requires regular exercise and access to the outdoors whilst a cat might be just as good company but wouldn't need exercise and could live in a flat or house with no garden. A caged bird can be good company and needs even less looking after than a cat. Even fish are better than nothing!

Breed

If you need a pet for exercise then probably only a dog will do, in which case you would be well advised to consider quite carefully which breed is likely to be most suitable. This may not be the same breed as you have chosen for most of your adult life. Smaller breeds are easier to control and generally cheaper to feed and maintain – but if too small, they may get under the feet of the elderly.

Age

Many people are daunted by the prospect of training and looking after a new puppy or kitten. On a practical level a person may be physically unable to clear up the mess left by a pet not yet housetrained, and there is always the danger of tripping over a small puppy or kitten, especially if your eyesight is poor.

Many people, therefore, adopt older pets, ones that are housetrained and fully grown. The main source of these is rescue kennels or an animal shelter. Many of the animals there have come from families who can no longer care for them and the kennels should be able to provide you with a suitable pet. Your vet might also know of a pet that needs a new home.

If you want to adopt an adult dog of a particular breed you can contact the appropriate breed rescue society but you should be careful to emphasise that you need a steady companion, not a problem dog in need of rehabilitation.

Impediments

In some cases the decision to replace your pet is taken away from you. If you live in sheltered accommodation you may find that the rules prevent you keeping any pet larger than a budgie or a goldfish. Losing a pet because one is obliged to rehome it can be as distressing as the pet actually dying. Some people have found that they could keep their pets until they died but that replacement was not allowed.

Arrangements for the future

As the benefits of pets in sheltered accommodation have become more widely recognised, attitudes towards pet ownership have softened – but not universally.

Many people decide not to get another pet because they feel they are too old to look after it properly and also because they fear that the pet will outlive them and face an uncertain future after their death. Naturally this is a very real concern. Some people approach this problem by stating their wishes in their will: one course of action is to arrange for the euthanasia of the pet, the other is to leave money to pay for its upkeep at an animal shelter or in the care of a trusted 'guardian'.

Another answer is the Cinnamon Trust, a charity whose main work is the care of animals whose owners have died or are terminally ill. Most of the Trust's work is with the elderly but they also extend help to younger terminally ill pet owners. The Trust runs an animal sanctuary and is also able, through local groups, to help look after pets of housebound people or people who are temporarily in hospital.

A case history

When Barbara's cat, Becky, died, Barbara decided not to replace her. She had first met Becky 15 years previously at a local animal shelter while she was searching for a cat that had gone missing several months before. She came across Becky, a tiny black and white ball of wailing fur and was convinced that the kitten would die if it stayed in the shelter another day. So she persuaded the shelter to let her take it home for a little TLC (tender loving care), promising to return it if its owners reappeared, which luckily for Barbara, they never did.

Barbara took Becky home and fed her with a baby's bottle until she was strong enough to manage on her own. The kitten survived and was soon going from strength to strength to become a loyal and loving companion. Barbara had another cat, Emma, but their relationship was never as close.

When she was six years old Becky started to show signs of asthma but responded well to treatment.

When she was 13, Becky became unwell and cried whenever she was picked up. A trip to the vet revealed two badly infected wounds, probably the result of a fight with another cat. The wounds were so infected that the vet advised that they be treated under a general anaesthetic. Barbara and the vet discussed Becky's asthma and both agreed that, although the anaesthetic was likely to be risky, it was a risk they had to take in Becky's best interests. If Becky didn't have the anaesthetic she would probably die from the infection.

The next day Barbara received a telephone call from her vet to tell her that Becky had suffered a fatal asthma attack as she was coming round from the anaesthetic.

Barbara was utterly devastated. Even though she knew of the risk she was unprepared for the shocking suddenness of Becky's death. She knew deep down that she had made the right decision but understandably she felt a sense of responsibility for Becky's death.

Barbara still has Emma, her other cat, 'Although I am naturally very fond of Emma, it just isn't the same.'

Becky will *never* be replaced because she was so special to Barbara. Their relationship was particularly close, partially because Barbara had rescued Becky and nursed her back to health and partially because Becky had been such a good companion as Barbara had aged and her own health had deteriorated.

Summary

1. A pet is often a vital link with the past.
2. Pets play an important role in the lives of the elderly.
3. The feelings of grief that an elderly person may feel when a pet dies may be intensified by renewed grieving for a dead spouse or friend.
4. The question of whether to replace is not easily resolved for the elderly.
5. The death of a pet can serve as a painful reminder that no-one is immortal.

Chapter 6

Euthanasia

A still small voice spake unto me,
'Thou art so full of misery,
Were it not better not to be?'

Alfred, Lord Tennyson, The Two Voices

Terminology

Making the decision

Subsequent emotions

The role of the vet

The right time

The place

Attendance

What happens

Possible problems

Payment

Summary

Terminology

The bereavement that we suffer on the death of a pet is similar in most ways to that we would suffer if a close friend or relative died.

However there is one aspect of bereavement following the death of a pet that is currently unique to pet owners: the special problems associated with euthanasia, which literally means 'easy death'.

There are many colloquial terms used to mean euthanasia:

- humane destruction
- put to sleep
- put down
- put out of misery

Such vague terms are, however, best avoided in favour of the straightforward word, euthanasia, especially as the other words can lead to serious misunderstandings and confusion, particularly where children are involved.

Euthanasia can be an active process in which positive steps are taken to end a life, or a passive process in which treatment is withheld in order to hasten death. Whilst passive euthanasia may occur in human medicine, active euthanasia is very rare and subject to much controversy.

In pet animals active euthanasia is commonly practised to prevent suffering in dying or incurable animals. The fact that active euthanasia is a positive act means that the pet owner is involved in making the decision.

Making the decision

Not surprisingly, whether or not to carry out euthanasia is a very difficult decision to make. It is a reversal of everything the caring pet owner has tried to do for all of the pet's life. Every decision they've ever made before was to improve and prolong their pet's life; now the ultimate decision is to end it.

How can you make such a decision? What if you're wrong? What's best for your pet may not be best for you.

Owners suddenly find their role changing from caretaker to decision-maker to executioner. It's the biggest responsibility an owner can be faced with and raises considerable moral issues. Is quality of life more important than quantity? Is taking any life morally acceptable?

As one owner faced with this problem commented: 'The underlying knowledge during the past year that I must sooner or later make a decision was very worrying to me. I had mixed feelings of grief, guilt and relief when the decision became inevitable.'

Subsequent emotions

Owners whose pet's life has been ended by euthanasia experience grief like all pet owners but they are particularly prone to feelings of guilt and anger.

❏ Guilt

Feelings of guilt are commonplace amongst owners in these cases, because ultimately it was they who made the decision. Was it the right decision? Was it too soon? Self doubt is always present even if the vet and all the owner's family and friends are sure that euthanasia was right and proper. Guilt is particularly likely to occur if the decision was partially an economic one. Deciding that you can't afford potentially life saving treatment is bound to make you feel uncomfortable and guilty.

❏ Anger

Anger is frequently directed at vets, largely because they're an obvious target. They 'murdered' your pet. They couldn't make it better. They *told* you to do it. They *made* you do it because you couldn't afford the treatment. They made a mistake.

Mistakes can happen even in the best practices, but sometimes they are imagined because the owner needs someone to blame to relieve his personal guilt.

Vets are aware of this need to blame someone and try not to take it personally if it's not deserved.

The decision-maker may be the subject of anger from other family members especially if they were not included in the decision making process. The decision-maker may be blamed simply for making a correct but unpopular decision, or the decision may be regarded as wrong or premature. Children can be very hurtful because they have difficulty differentiating between quantity and quality of life and they are often unable to understand that their parents might not be able to afford treatment.

The role of the vet

Who can help you make this decision? To some extent friends and relatives may help, they'll certainly have opinions and act as a yardstick of what is morally acceptable in your immediate social circle. However, the most important adviser will probably be your vet, who will serve as a vital source of information, being able to assess your pet's state of health and offer an opinion as to the degree of suffering involved, the probability of improvement and an estimate of your pet's remaining life span.

The vets' position may appear equivocal, whose side are they on? Their responsibility is to care for both you, the client and your pet, the patient. What's best for you may not best for your pet. All vets are primarily concerned with preventing animal suffering, that's why they became a vet.

Some people think that most vets are only too ready to end the lives of animals, but remember that euthanasia is very stressful for vets too. Vets find it particularly stressful to have to end the lives of healthy but unwanted stray animals, or of animals that are destroyed to suit their owners' convenience.

When an animal is nearing the end of its life it will become apparent that a decision will soon have to be made. In some cases a decision has to be taken about whether it is sensible to treat a potentially curable problem in an old animal. For some people there is no decision to make, the animal will be treated no matter what the cost or life expectancy. For others, probably the majority, it is necessary to balance the potential life expectancy against the likely suffering and the financial cost.

Major advances in medical and subsequently veterinary science have meant that it is possible to keep pets alive for longer; many previously incurable diseases are now curable, but at considerable expense. Owners may have to opt for euthanasia simply because they are unable or unwilling to pay; the anguish and guilt this can cause is considerable.

The right time

In most cases an animal's life is painlessly ended because it is suffering from an incurable disease. This raises the question of when an animal's quality of life has become inadequate.

Andrew Edney, a veterinary surgeon and past president of the British Small Animal Veterinary Association, has suggested a series of questions, noted below, which might help an owner or vet decide.

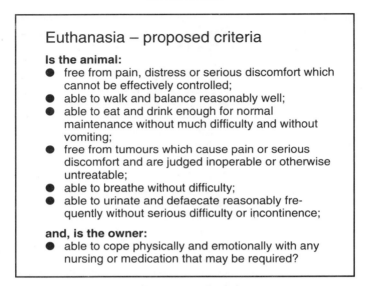

Euthanasia – proposed criteria

Is the animal:
- free from pain, distress or serious discomfort which cannot be effectively controlled;
- able to walk and balance reasonably well;
- able to eat and drink enough for normal maintenance without much difficulty and without vomiting;
- free from tumours which cause pain or serious discomfort and are judged inoperable or otherwise untreatable;
- able to breathe without difficulty;
- able to urinate and defaecate reasonably frequently without serious difficulty or incontinence;

and, is the owner:
- able to cope physically and emotionally with any nursing or medication that may be required?

If the answer to any of these questions is 'No' and treatment is unlikely to help, then euthanasia might be the preferred action to take.

❏ Talking to your vet

If you think that your pet has reached this stage, go and talk to your vet. It's not easy but try to explain that you think that euthanasia might be best for your pet and say why. In some cases you may be worrying unnecessarily; many conditions can be treated easily and cheaply these days and euthanasia may not be necessary.

For many people it is very difficult to recognise that a crisis has been reached; they can close their minds to the obvious. Some people are relieved if the vet broaches the subject of euthanasia; they may have brought the pet to the vet's with the firm intention of requesting euthanasia, but find themselves unable to make the request. Vets try their best to find out what their clients really want and talking frankly and openly can be a great help.

The role of the vet is to give you as good advice as possible. His job is not to make the decision for you but to help *you* make a decision and then support you and help you carry out that decision. It is quite rare for a vet to take a client to one side and say, 'Look, I know you're trying your best but further treatment can't help, the animal is suffering and I think you must allow me to let it die.'

Once you have decided that euthanasia is the right course of action, you and your vet will discuss when and where this will happen. In cases of chronic illness when the owner knows that euthanasia is a strong likelihood, euthanasia may be performed there and then. Remember, though, to ensure that everyone associated with the pet knows that this decision is likely to be made at that time and that they have been given the opportunity to prepare themselves.

On the other hand, if an apparently well pet is suddenly diagnosed as suffering from an incurable and fatal disease the owner will experience feelings of shocked disbelief. That owner and family need time to come to terms with the reality of the pet's illness and time to say goodbye. In situations like this, many vets prescribe some form of palliative treatment and suggest euthanasia as soon as things get any worse.

Certain criteria may be suggested to help owners accept the need for euthanasia and to decide when their pet's time has come. For example, the vet may suggest that euthanasia be carried out when the pet starts to vomit, becomes incontinent, etc.

The place

❏ At home

Most pet owners would prefer euthanasia to be carried out at home where the animal is in familiar surroundings. This is probably less distressing for the pet and also has several advantages for the owner: they don't suffer the embarrassment of showing grief in a public place and if the pet is to buried at home it doesn't need to be transported after death.

An owner who took this course of action described her feelings: 'Jessie was humanely destroyed at home. I was holding her and talking to her, I now find it comforting that this was the last thing she knew.'

Unfortunately some veterinary practices are unable or unwilling to provide this service because it is difficult in urban areas and is expensive in terms of time and manpower. Whilst this may be so, most practices know that this service is very important to their clients and therefore do their best to help. In some inner city areas, though, vets don't visit because they have been advised not to by the police.

Some vets are understandably less keen on euthanasia at home because it's often more difficult. To carry it out successfully most vets need the assistance of a trained helper; this may be unavailable at the owner's home at night or in an emergency or when euthanasia was not the expected outcome of the visit.

❏ At the surgery

Euthanasia is most commonly carried out at the vet's surgery because this is where most animals are examined, advice given and decisions made. The main advantages are that the surgery is usually well equipped and the vet can call on skilled help to ensure that everything goes smoothly with the minimum of distress for everyone.

The main disadvantage is that most owners see vets' surgeries as public places and no one wants to spend the last precious minutes with their pet waiting in a room full of people and apparently healthy animals. No one wants to cry in front of strangers.

'I took him to open surgery, we waited and waited, he seemed to be dying before my eyes. He had to be carried to the vet's room.'

If you know, or think you know, that euthanasia is necessary for your pet, you should try to mention this, if you feel you can, when you make the appointment. If you tell the receptionist it may be possible to arrange a time when no one else will be in the surgery so there'll be no waiting and no audience.

'I had an appointment with the vet when the general public were not in the surgery. I planned with my husband where our pet would be buried and prepared the place, we also took something to wrap her body in. All these preparations helped.'

Even if this isn't possible most vets are able to give you time and space both to say goodbye to your pet and compose yourself before you leave the surgery. Some surgeries even have a separate exit for you to use.

Attendance

The decision whether or not to be present is entirely yours, since vets will offer you the choice. Most people feel the need to be with their pet at the end; because their presence may be comforting to the pet, because they need to be sure that death was painless, that the pet is really dead and, above all, because they don't feel they can abandon their pet at the end.

Ultimately you must decide, but don't make yourself watch if you don't want to. Don't be swayed by what you think other people expect. It's worth bearing in mind, too, that if you're going to be really upset you might distress your pet who won't know what's happening, only that something's wrong.

If you can't be present when euthanasia is carried out, it is perfectly acceptable to ask to see the body immediately afterwards. Seeing the body enables you to say goodbye and it confirms in your mind that the pet is really dead.

Some owners experience problems if they don't do this because they never truly accept that death has occurred. 'I wish I had been offered the chance of being with him when he died. It upset me that I hardly had the chance to say goodbye to him properly before he was whisked away into another room.'

If you don't want to be present and you don't want to see the body you don't have to! Nobody at the surgery will think any the worse of you.

What happens

For most owners euthanasia is a terrible thing, not least because they may not know what is going to happen or what to expect. Those who have experienced it before will feel less confused.

Dogs and cats

In the UK, euthanasia of most cats and dogs is carried out by giving an injection of a strong barbiturate or a mixture of a barbiturate and other drugs into a vein. In very weak or collapsed animals the injection may be made into the abdominal cavity or an organ with a good blood supply like the kidney.

Injections are usually made into the vein which runs along the top of the animal's forearm. The animal has to be positioned so that the vet and the nurse can locate the vein and make the injection with the minimum of stress to the animal. This inevitably involves some degree of restraint, the degree naturally depends on the nature and training of the pet.

Whenever possible the vet wants the owner to be able to comfort and hold the pet but has to be mindful of personal safety as well as that of the staff and family witnesses. (In the USA owners sue vets if they get bitten by their own pet whilst it is undergoing treatment at the vet's!)

Most vets prefer the pet to be sitting or lying down, usually on a table. To help locate the vein, the vet will usually clip hair from a small area on your pet's leg. Surgical spirit is often used to clean the skin and make finding the vein easier. The nurse will hold your pet's leg and use a thumb as a tourniquet to 'raise' the vein. When everyone's ready the vet will insert the needle through the skin and into the vein, make sure that the needle is in the vein and then give the injection.

As the injection enters the bloodstream your pet will rapidly lose consciousness, become limp and lie down. Breathing will stop almost immediately and then the heart will stop beating. From the moment your pet loses consciousness it is no longer aware of anything although you may see muscles twitching for some minutes after the injection. You should be prepared for older animals to take longer to drift off into unconsciousness because their circulation is slower. Most animals tend to urinate and pass faeces after they lose consciousness because the muscles controlling the bladder and anus relax. Dogs and cats don't close their eyes after death.

It is not uncommon for an animal that has stopped breathing to gasp after a few minutes. This is *not* a sign of life but simply a reflex action. Most vets will warn owners about this in advance because it can be very upsetting if a pet that appears to be dead suddenly shows 'signs of life'.

After a short while your vet will check that your pet's heart has stopped but he'll stay with you until all muscular activity has stopped and there is no chance of gasping occurring.

If euthanasia took place at the surgery your vet will probably offer you the chance to be alone with your pet afterwards. If you want, you'll be able to talk to one of the nurses. You may be offered a cup of tea (you may not want it); it can't bring your dog back but it's a gesture of sympathy and it shows that they're trying to help.

If you're at home the vet will probably leave as soon as your pet is definitely dead because he will not want to intrude on your grief.

Horses

Traditionally horses' lives are ended by being shot. Whilst death following shooting is instantaneous, painless and humane, it can be very distressing for the owner. It is becoming increasingly common for euthanasia of horses to be performed by the injection of strong barbiturates. This form of euthanasia takes longer and is considerably more expensive than shooting, but is immeasurably less distressing for the owner. After euthanasia by injection, the horse's body can be disposed of by burial or cremation – it cannot be used for meat.

Consent forms

Before they carry out euthanasia, most vets will ask you to read and sign a consent form which states in plain language that your pet's life is to be brought to an end. Most people realise that this is a necessary formality but naturally some feel that it's like signing a 'death warrant' or consider it to be an intrusion on their grief.

Consent forms are necessary to protect the vet in case an owner changes his mind and denies giving permission, or if there are disputes about ownership of the pet. Sometimes one family member will request euthanasia and other members may disagree later. Owners may even deny giving permission or claim that they didn't understand what they were signing in order to escape the blame. Consent forms cannot be signed by minors and vets will invariably refuse to carry out enthanasia of an animal brought to the surgery by an unaccompanied child.

Disposal

If euthanasia was carried out at your home and your vet is going to dispose of your pet's body it will have to be taken back to the surgery. The body will be placed in a hygienic, impervious container, usually a strong plastic sack. Although your vet knows this may be distressing to you, it is necessary because it is usual for a recently dead animal to pass both urine and faeces and vets are required by health and safety regulations to prevent any risks to staff arising from handling the bodies of dead pets.

A pet that is left at the surgery for disposal will ultimately have to be placed in a similar container but your vet is unlikely to distress you by doing this in your presence. If you're taking your pet home to bury it the vet will offer you a bag or a plastic sheet to protect your car on the way home.

Possible problems

In an ideal world everything goes smoothly and the service you receive will be professional, skilful and sympathetic. Unfortunately things don't always go as planned and anything that does go wrong greatly increases the distress experienced by an owner.

Most problems occur if there is difficulty making the injection. Repeated attempts to locate a vein can be distressing for both pet and owner. Sometimes a pet is so ill that it is very difficult for the vet to locate a vein. Similar difficulties can occur if the pet is in pain and resists any form of handling. Sedating a pet beforehand can help calm a very nervous animal but often has the unwanted effect of making the vein harder to find. Sometimes the vet is simply less experienced. 'It took a long time to find a vein, he (the vet) was obviously nervous and we all suffered from his inexperience'.

An owner may be upset if the pet needs to be rather firmly restrained, and especially if it needs to be muzzled. Most vets do not routinely muzzle pets for euthanasia, but they have a duty to protect themselves, their staff, the public and you the owner. Vets seldom get bitten by dogs that bite, only by ones that 'have never bitten anyone before'!

It is upsetting if an animal makes a noise or groans as it loses consciousness as this might suggest that the animal was in pain or aware of what was happening. However, this is most unlikely to be the case, as unconsciousness occurs rapidly. The noise is most likely made by air escaping from the lungs as the animal lies down.

It can also be upsetting if more than one injection is needed to produce death. The dose of barbiturate needed to cause rapid death does vary between individuals, so occasionally a second dose will be required. Very large pets may need a bigger volume than can be conveniently administered in a single injection. However, remember that consciousness is lost very quickly after the *first* injection so your pet will be unaware of the additional injection even though you are.

Some animals seem to take a long while to die. The main causes of this are slow circulation in old or ill animals, or not all the injection going into the vein because the animal wriggled at a critical moment. Never forget, though, that at a time of crisis – and euthanasia is a time of crisis – time can appear to slow down considerably.

Less commonly some people are shocked by how quickly the injection works. This can be avoided if the vet discusses with the owner, in advance, what is going to happen.

'I imagined the vet would inject her and I'd take her home still alive and she'd not wake up. I hadn't realised that she'd die there and then.'

It seems only too easy for vets and their staff to appear unsympathetic. At a time of great emotional stress people become particularly sensitive to everything that goes on around them and it is very easy for a chance remark made by the vet or staff to become magnified and misinterpreted. When a vet says, sympathetically, 'It's a shame, he looks so well otherwise,' an owner who has doubts might take this to mean that the vet doesn't agree with his decision.

Payment

Euthanasia is a professional service provided by veterinary surgeons and like all services it needs to be paid for. The problem arises, though, that no one wants to demand money from a grieving owner immediately after their pet's death. To avoid this, some owners pay in advance so that they don't have to pay at the time or receive an account later. In practice, if an owner doesn't offer to pay at the time, most vets will wait a decent interval and then send an account.

'We were told we didn't have to pay at the time, but could come back in a few days time, however we opted to pay and get it over with. This was seen to by one of the nurses and we were able to leave through a side door as the vet thought it better for us, rather than facing the other people in the waiting room.'

If you are not an established client of a veterinary practice you must expect to pay at the time. It may seem insensitive but it's a reflection of how many people abuse the system and don't pay their bills.

Summary

The decision to agree to euthanasia of their pet is a major responsibility that many owners have to face.

1. Always discuss the decision with other family members.
2. Discuss with your vet when, where and how euthanasia is to be performed.
3. The decision to be present or not is yours alone.
4. A basic knowledge of what will happen during euthanasia will probably reduce your distress to some degree.

Chapter 7

The final resting place

Under the wide and starry sky
Dig the grave and let me lie.
Glad did I live and gladly die,
– And I laid me down with a will.
This is the verse you grave for me:
'Here he lies where he longed to be;
Home is the sailor, home from the sea,
And the hunter home from the hill.'

                        Robert Louis Stevenson, Underwoods

Deciding where

Home burial

Burial in a pet cemetary

Cremation

Funerals

Tributes to your pet's memory

Afterthought

Summary

Deciding where

The death of a pet doesn't only bring emotional problems, it can also bring practical ones. Arranging for the disposal of your pet's body can cause additional distress at what is already a traumatic time. At the time when a pet dies most owners are so distressed that they find it difficult to make decisions and frequently, once the initial shock wears off, owners wish they had acted differently.

If you anticipate the imminent death of your pet you can discuss disposal with your vet before your pet dies. The vet will be able to give you some idea of the services available locally and help you to make a decision in advance. Having time to think about your decision means that you're much more likely to make the right one and less likely to suffer regret later.

Deciding what to do with your pet's remains is a very personal thing. Most people need to feel assured that their pet's body was treated with dignity and respect and many people are prepared to go to considerable effort and expense to ensure this.

Making this sort of a decision is often a family matter; the majority of pets live in a family and it is, therefore, advisable to consult all the parties involved.

Be prepared for your decisions to be criticised by friends and relatives. Many people wouldn't see the point of spending time and money on the disposal of a pet and commemorating its memory. Ignore them! When a human dies large sums of money are spent on the funeral because a human *has* to be buried or cremated. When a pet dies you dispose of its body with care and dignity because you *want* to.

It isn't necessary to spend a lot of money: love, care and dignity are the main requirements at the end of a pet's life. The important thing is to do what feels right for you. If you feel entirely happy with the way that your pet's body was treated then you may find that the grief that accompanies its death is easier to bear.

Home burial

A common, but declining, means of disposing of a pet's body is burial at home in the garden. The acute sense of loss and separation that follows the death of a pet may be lessened by knowing that your pet's remains are close by. Being able to visit the grave and talk to your pet whenever you feel the urge can be helpful to the grieving process. Furthermore, the fact that you can see a grave in the garden can help you to accept the reality of your pet's death. The sight of the grave may cause emotional pain initially but in time it usually brings comfort.

Home burial may well stir up a variety of apparently strange emotions; some people feel a temptation to dig their pet up again just to hold it one more time, others may experience feelings of anger and resentment when it rains or gets cold. These feelings are quite natural, a response to the death that will pass in time.

A burial at home is an active process. It is something that you, the owner, have to plan and do yourself. Most people like to bury a pet near its favourite place in the garden. People who don't have a garden, who want to bury their pet but don't want to use a pet cemetery, may well find that they can bury their pet in a friend's or neighbour's garden.

Home burial does, however, pose some practical problems in that it is not easy to dig to the required depth of 1.25m.

❏ Common questions about home burial

Q My dog is too big to bury, but I want him near me. What can I do?

A You could have him cremated and then bury the ashes in your garden.

Q I am not physically able to dig a grave myself, who might help?

A A friend or neighbour may help you, and there are companies that will undertake to bury your pet at home. As noted earlier, digging to an adequate depth can be difficult in many cases.

Q I want to bury my cat in his favourite spot, but my husband disagrees, as he is going to alter the layout of the garden. What can we do?

A It might be better to choose another spot then your husband will not have to worry about disturbing the grave.

Q Is it safe to bury my cat anywhere in the garden?

A Yes, up to a point. You should avoid mains cables and service pipes.

Q I'm unsure whether to bury my cat in the garden, because I will be moving shortly. What alternatives are availabe?

A If you have your cat cremated, you can keep the ashes until you are able to bury them in the new garden.

Q I would like a casket to bury my dog in, where can I obtain one?

A Several pet cremation services offer a range of caskets suitable for all sizes. Also, a local undertaker may have something suitable for your dog.

Q Will people think I am silly if I bury a reminder of myself with my pet?

A No, it is quite acceptable to bury something like an old jumper or even a favourite toy with your pet. Although this gesture is obviously mainly symbolic, it can be comforting.

Q I live in the country. Can you suggest a way of preventing wild animals from digging up my dog's grave?

A You could cover the grave with paving slabs or heavy quarry stones. If done properly, this can look attractive as well as being practical. Make sure, too, that the grave is quite deep, about 3 or 4 ft (1.25m).

Q What could I have as a memorial for my cat?

A Trees and shrubs make lovely memorials to pets. Also, a wide selection of headstones and plaques are available from pet crematoria or masonry firms who advertise in the popular animal press.

Q My daughter does not want to attend the 'funeral' of the family dog. Should I make her?

A No – you should never force anyone to attend a burial. Your daughter may want to say goodbye to the dog in her own way, and in her own time.

❏ Subsequent house moves

In an uncertain world a change of job or personal circumstances may mean that you have to move house. If you have buried a much loved pet in your garden, especially if its death was recent, you may not want to leave the pet behind and the thought of moving can become a nightmare. If you find yourself in this situation there are several things you can do to help yourself.

- When you move to your new house you can allocate a part of your new garden as a garden of remembrance. You can plant a tree or shrub or erect a memorial, a stone plaque perhaps. You could even bury a personal reminder of your pet, a collar or toy for example.
- When you sell your home explain to the new owners about your pet's grave. Show them where it is in the hope that they will respect your wishes and not accidentally disturb the grave. You could also place a stone or slab to mark the grave site. Not all new owners will understand or respect your request and not every one wants to know that there is a grave in their garden, but it is still worth asking.
- If possible, try to tell yourself that what you buried in your garden were your pet's remains, his discarded shell. The memory of his love and devotion will live on forever in your heart, wherever you live.

Burial in a pet cemetery

Pet cemeteries are particularly useful for those owners who would like to bury their pet's body or ashes but are unable to do so at home.

Some people don't have a garden or are not allowed to bury their pet. Other people may be about to move house when their pet dies and they would prefer to use a pet cemetery because they will be able to visit the grave after they move. Some owners choose a pet cemetery because they want to, because they would like to commemorate their pet's life and death in a more formal way.

There are pet cemeteries in most parts of the country; your vet will probably know which ones are nearest to you. There are not many pet cemeteries and so the nearest one may be some distance away.

When you are choosing a pet cemetery it is definitely a good idea to visit it first to see for yourself if it seems right for you. Some cemeteries are formal with the graves close together, others are more informal with the graves spread over a landscaped garden of remembrance.

Pet cemeteries are usually able to offer a very personal and sympathetic service. They can provide a wide range of services from a simple burial to an elaborate funeral. The cemetery can collect your pet from your home or the vet's surgery, especially if you don't have your own transport or you are unable to do this yourself. The cemetery will prepare the grave and help you to bury your pet. In addition the cemetery can supply simple coffins to hold the body and a suitable memorial to mark the grave. Some pet cemeteries can even organise a simple memorial service at the time of burial.

Burial in a pet cemetery is usually the most expensive way to dispose of your pet's remains. The cost will vary widely depending on where you live and on how elaborate your plans are. You may also find that there is an annual maintenance fee to pay as well.

Most pet cemeteries are well run by responsible people, many are owned by people who found that they were unable to get the service they wanted when their own pets died.

On a cautionary note, though, there is no national code of practice covering the way in which a pet cemetery is run. Unlike human cemeteries, pet cemeteries are not built on consecrated ground. This means that your pet's grave might be at risk if the company operating the cemetery went out of business. It is also worth checking if your pet's grave is permanent or whether it will be cleared and re-used after a number of years.

In the UK, burial in a pet cemetery is the least used option for disposing of a pet's remains. In the USA pet cemeteries are more widely used for the simple reason that many US cities have local laws forbidding burial at home.

Cremation

An increasing number of pets are cremated when they die. Cremation is dignified, hygienic and practical. There are two main ways in which this can be done: either the pet is cremated on its own and its ashes returned to the owner, or the pet is cremated communally with several other pets.

❏ Communal cremation

Most pets that are routinely disposed of by vets are cremated communally. The pets' bodies are collected and cremated by a local pet crematorium. Between the death of a pet and its cremation, its body will be preserved by refrigeration. Normally the pet crematorium will visit the veterinary surgery once or twice a week and your pet will be cremated within a few days of its death.

As several pets are cremated together it isn't possible to have an individual pet's ashes returned. Usually the pet crematorium will dispose of the ashes from communal cremations by burying them in the crematorium grounds. Cremation in this way is a decent, no frills service, a basic one aimed to help bereaved pet owners solve a difficult practical problem at minimal expense.

Not all vets use a pet crematorium to dispose of pets' remains and so when you arrange for a vet to dispose of your pet's body it pays to ask what method is used and to make different arrangements if you wish.

Some people are either too upset or too embarrassed to ask their vet what will actually happen to their pet's body. This uncertainty can lead to serious problems later and can prevent owners from resolving their grief. If you want to know, you should ask; your vet will not be offended. What happens to the pets' bodies in the practice is not a secret, it would be unprofessional conduct if your vet tried to mislead you.

Often, owners who left their pet with their vet like to visit the crematorium later to see for themsleves what happend to their pet. Other owners do not want to know any details about the disposal of their pet, who would rather draw a blind over the entire episode. There are also owners who don't attach any importance whatsoever to the fate of their pets' bodies after death.

❏ Individual cremation

For owners wishing their pet to be cremated but wanting something more than the anonymity of communal cremation it is always possible to arrange for individual cremation.

An individual cremation will be more expensive than communal cremation but the reassurance gained from knowing exactly what happened to their pet can be so comforting that for some people this is the ideal choice. Other advantages can also be listed:

- The owner has the assurance that the ashes are those of their pet alone. Most pet crematoria issue certificates to confirm this.
- The pet crematorium will usually collect your pet's body from the vet's surgery or your home on the day you contact them and make arrangements. Your pet will not be kept for several days before it is cremated.

As with pet cemeteries, most pet crematoria offer a range of services enabling the bereaved owner to select what seems most appropriate for their pet.

One family was very distressed when Lady, their ageing Old English Sheepdog, became acutely ill. After several days with no signs of improvement, they reluctantly decided that euthaniasia was the only answer to Lady's suffering.

Naturally, the family was extremely upset, and even more so when they discovered it would be several days before Lady's body would be collected from their vet for cremation. 'I just couldn't bear to drive past knowing she was in there.'

In the end they rang the pet crematorium directly to find out about other services available. 'It was such a relief to hand it all over to someone else; we just couldn't cope ourselves.'

Lady's body was collected that evening from their home and the next day she was cremated. The family were able to attend, to say their final goodbyes and take the ashes home with them in a casket. They buried this under their pet's favourite tree.

Choosing a crematorium can be difficult since standards at this time are variable. It makes sense to ask the questions noted below to help ensure that you will be satisfied and that the service will meet your particular requirements and remember that you can visit crematoria before the event.

Questions to ask about individual cremation

- Are you able to be present at the cremation?
- Will the crematorium collect your pet's remains straightaway, with dignity and in a suitable vehicle?
- Can you take your pet's remains directly to the crematorium?
- Is the service provided dignified and caring?
- How much will everything cost – collection, cremation and an appropriate container for ashes?

- Can you have the ashes buried or scattered at the crematorium? How much would this cost? Is there a maintenance fee for burial?
- In what sort of container will ashes be returned?
- Will you get a certificate guaranteeing that your pet was individually cremated and that the ashes are solely those of your pet?
- Does the crematorium keep proper records of all the pets it cremates?
- Are the staff sympathetic, helpful, open and frank?

❏ Horses

Many horse owners are extremely distressed when their horse dies, and they too face a difficult problem when it comes to disposing of the remains. Traditionally, horses' bodies are used as a source of meat for pet foods or, overseas, for human consumption. This is clearly unsatisfactory for many bereaved horse owners. There are two main alternatives: burial or cremation.

Burial is only possible if you have enough land to accommodate a grave – and you may need specialist advice to do this properly.

It is now possible in the UK to have your horse cremated. Good pet crematoria are equipped to collect and cremate horses' bodies and this can provide the best solution to a difficult problem.

❏ Pre-payment

In order to spread the cost of cremating a pet, or arranging its burial in a pet cemetery, some pet crematoria and cemeteries offer prepayment plans. These enable you to make funeral plans in advance and to start saving towards the cost.

Funerals

When a human dies it is usual for there to be a funeral. This normally takes the form of a religious service in which the dead person's qualities are praised and his life remembered. A gathering of people mourning the death can be a great comfort to those close friends and relatives who are most severely affected by grief. In addition a funeral provides a time to say goodbye to the dead person. Acknowledging that a person is dead and can never return is a vital part of the grieving process.

In a similar way a funeral service for a pet plays a vital role in enabling bereaved pet owners to come to terms with their loss and complete the grieving process. Pet owners who never really accept the loss of their pet often find that they are unable to resolve their feelings of grief.

A funeral service for a pet need be no more than a simple act of remembrance that can be shared by the pet's immediate family. It is a last chance for everyone to say goodbye and an opportunity for the bereaved owners to recognise and share each other's grief.

The burial of your pet's body or ashes is a natural time for this to take place. Even if you don't have anything to bury it is still possible to allocate a time to remember your pet's life and death.

When a pet goes missing there comes a time when you have to acknowledge that it is lost forever even though you will never know its fate. Deciding to perform an act of remembrance may help you to come terms with this uncertainty and enable you to complete the grieving process.

Some form of funeral is particularly important when a family pet dies, especially if young children are involved. Young children often don't understand that death is a permanent state and seeing a pet buried can help them to realise that it will never come back. Children and young adults are also inclined to hide their feelings of grief for fear of being ridiculed. If they can see that other family members are upset, this will help them to express their feelings rather than bottling them up.

Attendance at a pet's funeral should be optional, no-one should be forced to attend.

A prayer on the death or loss of a pet

Dear Lord

All animals are part of Your creation. Thank You for the life of (—) and for all the love and companionship we have shared. Nothing can separate us from the memories of his/her time among us and we feel richer for having known him/her. We now entrust him/her to Your keeping, O Lord, knowing that You will care for him/her in Your special and loving way.

Amen   *Gill Ponting*

Tributes to your pet's memory

Many pet owners feel that they want to honour their pet's memory in a permanent way. This is a way of extending contact with a pet and making sure that it is not forgotten. It can be a great comfort to bereaved pet owners to know that there is a long-lasting, tangible reminder of their pet.

Gravestones

The most obvious way to do this is to erect a gravestone or plaque over the grave. Even if there is no actual grave it is still possible to have a memorial in the garden where your pet used to play. There are now a number of companies that specialise in creating pet memorials; you can usually find their advertisements in dog and cat magazines. Memorials to pets are not a recent idea; many large country houses have small pet cemeteries in their grounds. There is even a pet cemetery in the grounds of Edinburgh castle where dogs belonging to the garrison are buried.

Living memorials

Some people would prefer to have a living thing as a memorial to their pet and so plant a tree or shrub, usually at the site of the grave. If this isn't possible, it may be acceptable to sponsor the planting of a tree by a nature conservation group such as the Woodland Trust. People without a garden could buy a long lived indoor plant as a form of living memorial to their pet.

Donations

When a pet dies it is possible to commemorate it in a way that benefits other animals. A donation can be given to one of the animal welfare charities to help prevent suffering in animals or to help treat animals whose owners can't afford proper veterinary treatment. Alternatively you can donate medical equipment or money towards clinical research that might eventually help to cure animals suffering from the same disease that affected your pet.

Reminders

A memorial is a public reminder of your pet but most people like to keep something more personal as a reminder too.

When your pet dies you will probably find that at first, any reminders cause you pain and you may be tempted to throw everything away to avoid this. However, once the initial feelings of acute grief start to fade, you may find that you can gain great comfort from having reminders around to touch, see and smell. Because of this it is advisable to put your pet's things away until you feel ready to face them again. If you don't want to keep them you can then throw them away or give them to someone who can use them.

People like to keep a variety of reminders of their pets. Most of us have photographs of our pets; when a pet dies it is possible to have one or two special pictures mounted in frames. Some people have a portrait of their pet painted, either from life or from a photograph. You will find that pet artists advertise in the dog and cat magazines. More recently people have been able to make films or video recordings of their pets when they were alive and well.

Lots of people keep collars, leads, brushes and toys as reminders. Some people will keep hair, whiskers and even occasionally teeth.

A reminder of your pet is a very personal thing. What may comfort you may be very distressing to someone else. In situations where there was more then one owner of the pet a compromise may have to be reached regarding what reminders of the pet are kept and how they are located or displayed around the house.

Afterthought

All people react differently to death and everyone has different views and beliefs. The important thing to ensure is that your pet's remains are treated in accordance with your wishes and expectations. The final task of laying your pet to rest should be undertaken in a manner that is comforting and acceptable to you.

Summary

1. Try to decide in advance how you would like to dispose of your pet's body.
2. Do what you and your immediate family feel is right, don't be swayed by other people's opinions.
3. Do have a funeral, especially if you have children.
4. A memorial to your pet is not only a reminder, it helps you to accept the reality of your pet's death.
5. Don't discard all reminders of your pet, although painful at first, they may become a comfort as time passes.

Chapter 8

Loss without a body

Then from the wood a voice cried, 'Ah, in vain
In vain I seek thee, O thou bitter sweet;
In what lone land are set thy longed-for feet?'
William Morris, Missing, A book of verse

Special problems

Learning to cope

Searching for missing pets

Identification of pets

Rehoming

Summary

Special problems

❏ Lack of understanding

When a pet dies you may receive some sympathy from family and friends. They probably know that you loved the pet and to a certain extent they may be able to understand your sadness at its death. When a pet goes missing, you may encounter a very different reaction from those around you. Because the loss is intangible, friends and relatives may well be unaware of the devastating effect the disappearance of your pet has had on you.

People may sympathise with the death of a pet or express horror at an accidental death, but when there is no illness, no accident and no body, they may find it difficult to comprehend the feelings of loss and distress experienced by the owner.

'My immediate family were upset, but other friends and relatives were quite without compassion and I was deeply hurt. I felt that I had somehow lost more than my cat.'

This owner desperately needed support and recognition of her loss, but she was acutely aware that it wasn't forthcoming from people around her.

❏ Uncertainty

When a pet disappears the pain it causes can be never-ending for the owner. The uncertainty of not knowing what has happened is often worse than the reality of death. Unfortunately many pet owners have to face the fact that they may never see their animal again.

'I let my dog out at 10 o'clock. It was normal for him to run in the woods at the back of the house for ten minutes every evening. That was the last time I ever saw him. I can't cope with not knowing what happened to him.'

But why does a pet going missing hurt so much? The feelings of bereavement experienced when a pet dies are largely due to the involuntary breaking of the emotional bonds between you and your pet. If your pet disappears, the relationship is shattered just as surely.

This loss is compounded by the awful uncertainty of its fate. Is your pet alive or dead? Is it happy, sad or frightened? If it's dead, did it suffer? The list of unanswerable questions is endless and we can all imagine ourselves in a similar situation.

This uncertainty is a major block to the process of grieving. How can you grieve for an animal that may or may not be dead! If you can't start you can't stop and many people suffer from unresolved feelings of grief years later.

One little cat went missing and despite massive searches and much advertising was never found. Even a year later the owner was still hoping that it would return. The owner found that she was having great difficulty accepting her loss because, unlike previous times when her pets had died, this time she had not been given 'the opportunity to mourn my missing pet'.

In one way a missing pet is upsetting because it stirs up deep fears of abandonment and this is especially true for children: if the dog can disappear who will be next, mum or dad?

❏ Anger and guilt

As with pet death, anger and guilt are often components of the grieving process. Some animals will wander off quite voluntarily and regularly. If you know that your pet falls into this category then you should be extra vigilant when letting your pet out and you should try not to let it out unsupervised.

If you don't supervise your pet outside and it does wander off then you must expect to shoulder some of the blame. Although you may be angry with the pet for running off and angry with yourself for giving it the opportunity, you should turn your energies towards looking for it.

If it's a family pet, it's better to discuss the loss as a family: get the guilt, blame and recriminations out into the open. This will probably enable everyone to cope and then work as one to look for the pet.

❏ No goodbyes

When a pet dies we usually have a chance to say 'goodbye'. If a pet goes missing this is clearly impossible. 'I couldn't believe that I would never see my beautiful white cat again, one minute she was in the garden, then she had disappeared from my life forever; I never said goodbye to her.'

Helping people whose pet has disappeared

- Although it is difficult to understand an intangible loss, try to respect the pet owner's feelings.
- Offer support and give people the opportunity to talk about their pet.
- Encourage them to talk about their relationship with their pet and don't be embarrassed by their tears.

❏ Stolen pets

Jackie had owned her pony since she was four years old. When she was 28 he disappeared from his field one night and was never seen again. Despite inquiries and extensive media appeals no trace of the pony was ever found.

After 24 years it was only natural that a very strong bond had existed between the two of them and Jackie was devastated. She found that she regularly dreamt about her horse and that she couldn't pass a field without looking over the hedge, 'hoping to find him'.

'If only I knew whether is he alive or dead. Was he treated cruelly or is someone, somewhere, loving him as I did?

'I sometimes wish that he had died of old age; I could have accepted that. It is the uncertainty that is the most difficult to come to terms with.'

Learning to cope

When a pet has been missing for a long time it may be helpful to perform a simple act of memorial in acknowledgement of your loss. Although there isn't a body to bury it is still possible to commemorate your pet with, perhaps, a small bush or tree as a tribute. Even if you live in a flat and don't have a garden, a long-lasting indoor plant can serve the same purpose. A memorial is an important step towards letting go of your emotional ties to your pet. It is a way of saying goodbye and giving yourself permission to start grieving. This is a major step towards accepting your loss and subsequently towards the resolution of your grief.

Memorials are particularly important for children to help them understand that the pet will not return. Younger children's concept of death is hazy, their concept of a pet going missing is likely to be more so.

Different people are bound to cope differently when their pet goes missing. In time some people accept that the pet is dead, others prefer to believe that the pet strayed and is living safely with another family. Others will continue to search for months, even years, afterwards just in case their pet reappears out of the blue.

Some people never fully accept the loss of their missing pet. They will always nurture a secret hope that one day the pet will return safe and sound. If such a hope helps you to cope with your loss then all is well. However if you find yourself depending on this hope and living your life around it then all is not well.

You should try to put your loss into perspective and attempt to be realistic about the improbability of the outcome you desire. It is quite usual to leave the pet's bowls and belongings around the house for some time afterwards. Eventually as you learn to accept the loss you can put these sad reminders away for the last time.

You can't supervise a pet every second of its life and unexpected things can happen to anyone. As one owner said: 'Since then I haven't had the confidence to allow my cats to roam freely and I have made them safe and healthy prisoners in my home.'

Learning to cope – a check list

- Do as much as you reasonably can to find your pet.
- If, after a certain length of time, there is no trace of your pet, try to accept your loss.
- Acknowledge to yourself that you may *never* know what has happened to your pet.
- Perform a simple act as a memorial to your pet: plant a tree or shrub or place a headstone in your garden. This is both a tribute to your missing pet and provides a time to say goodbye. Some people may prefer to make a donation to an animal charity in memory of their pet.
- Give yourself permission to grieve and when you think you have grieved enough give yourself permission to stop.
- Allow yourself time to adjust to your loss and to the uncertainty.

Searching for missing pets

Check favourite places

When a pet disappears the first thing to do is to check the place where the pet was last seen and all its usual favourite haunts and walks. Naturally it pays to visit these places more than once but it is unreasonable to search time and time again.

Peter accidentally lost his dog at the seaside. Later the same day he returned and searched fruitlessly until it got dark. Despairing he returned to his car only to find the dog patiently waiting for him. This story has a happy ending, unfortunately a lot don't.

Advertise

If initial searches prove fruitless it helps to advertise by placing notices in local shops, veterinary surgeries and newspapers, putting posters on trees near where the pet disappeared, even appealing on local radio.

In all cases you should give as detailed a description of your pet as possible: breed, colour, sex, age, in fact anything that might help to identify it. Good quality photographs can be particularly useful. If your pet is insured you may find that the policy offers money towards the cost of advertising and recovery.

Useful contacts

Important contacts are the local police as quite a number of dogs are taken to police stations by the public. The police will also be aware of any road accidents involving dogs because motorists are legally required to report such accidents. Unfortunately this is not the case with cats and the police have no responsibilities for controlling stray or lost cats. All dogs taken to police stations are handed over to local authorities who will keep a stray dog for seven days and then dispose of it either by rehoming or euthanasia.

Most people ring local veterinary surgeries to see if their pet has been found dead or injured. Vets will usually give first aid treatment to injured stray animals that are brought to their surgeries; they know that most animals belong to someone and will be claimed in a day or two. In the absence of an owner, the RSPCA may pay for initial treatment and arrange for an unclaimed animal to be rehomed. It may be necessary to carry out euthanasia on seriously injured animals without the owner's permission, to prevent further suffering.

It is important to check all the local animal shelters, especially if you've lost a dog. It is better to visit the kennels rather than describe your pet over the telephone. We have heard of a number of people who have been assured that no dogs fitting their pet's description have been admitted to the kennels only to find it was there all the time. Visit the kennels several times during the first fortnight after the disappearance and note that kennels are only required to keep dogs for seven days.

Sometimes if your pet has been killed in a road accident passers by may move or dispose of the body. Because of this the owner may never learn of the pet's fate and, as already described, the uncertainty that this causes is very damaging.

'I checked all her usual favourite places and then, on the way home, I saw what I thought was a black plastic bag sticking out from under a hedge. At first it was curiosity that drew me nearer, then absolute horror as I realised that I was looking at the black paw of my Scottie.'

Despite the obvious unpleasantness of finding her pet in this way, the owner was comforted by the fact that at least she knew for certain what had happened. She had her dog back and she was able to bury him in her garden. This gave her the opportunity to say goodbye and begin grieving.

Finding dead pets

If you should *find* a dead pet on the road, by all means move it to the curb, but do look for any signs of identification and if possible place notices in local shops or on nearby trees. If you do this you could be saving someone a lot of unnecessary worry.

Identification of pets

No matter what the ultimate fate of your pet you can greatly increase your chances of recovering it or confirming its death by ensuring that it can be identified at all times. If an injured pet can be immediately identified you will be informed and you can then ensure that it will receive appropriate emergency treatment promptly.

- The cheapest and simplest way to identify a pet is with an **engraved disc** or something similar attached to its collar. This is a legal requirement in the UK for all dogs over six months of age. The discs can carry the dog's name, the owner's address or simply their telphone number. Wood Green Animal Shelter runs a computerised scheme for linking pets and their owners and issue a special dog disc engraved with a personal reference number. This scheme has proven to be extremely effective. Some people are worried that collars are dangerous on cats because they might become caught on trees and fences. Whilst this is possible the risk is very slight.
  Advantage: a disc can be read and understood by anyone.
  Disadvantages: the disc may wear smooth, and it is all too easy for a collar to fall off or be removed by a thief.

- A permanent means of identification is to **tattoo** a unique identity number on the pet's skin.
  Advantage: it is indelible and hard to tamper with.
  Disadvantages: tattoos are frequently illegible and a number means nothing on its own. In order to identify the owner it is necessary to identify where the dog is registered (there are several registers) and then ring the register. Attempts are currently being made to produce a single national register of dogs and owners.

- The latest method of identifying animals is the **Identichip**, an electronic device the size of a grain of rice that is injected beneath an animal's skin. When the device is interrogated by a special detector it transmits its unique identity number which is displayed on a screen. A telephone call to the computerised register will enable the owner of the animal to be located.
  Advantages: the system is tamperproof, permanent and suitable for most animals including dogs, cats and horses.
  Disadvantages: a special detector is needed to read the chip and these are not to be found in all vets, rescue kennels and police stations. A further complication is that there are several different types of chip, each needing different makes of detector. It can also be difficult to find where the chip is, as they sometimes move under the skin. Detection can also be difficult in wet dogs.

- There are other permanent methods of identification available, for instance ear studs which again are numbered and the numbers stored on a computer.

Rehoming

Loss without a body does not only cover the unsolved disappearance of your pet. It can also include those occasions when for one reason or another an owner has to find another home for a valued and loved pet. Despite the fact that the owner knows that the pet is alive and well, the feelings experienced will be those of bereavement.

The animal is not dead but the emotional bond has been painfully broken. Outsiders can be unsympathetic, all they see is that the animal is alive and well, that you gave the animal away apparently of your own volition and that you seem to be unreasonably upset. 'After all it's not as though it's really dead,' is a common remark that will come from family and friends.

Whilst no one gives away their pet willingly, in most cases there is a degree of choice. The fact that you are faced with choice causes feelings of guilt if you feel you are letting your pet down – even betraying its trust in you. Owners may also feel anger that they have been forced by fate into the role of decision maker.

In some cases the decision to rehome a pet brings positive advantages to the owner; for example, enabling acceptance of a new job overseas. In other circumstances the decision may be necessary to prevent disadvantages, e.g. it may be necessary because the pet has bitten one of the children. At either extreme there is at least some benefit to be gained that can be set against the pain and the guilt.

❏ Duration of grief

Grieving for a pet which has died can be prolonged, grieving for a pet that is not dead can be interminable. It can be very difficult to sever the emotional bonds, especially if you know where the pet is living, and particularly if the new owners keep you informed of its health and happiness. Constant reminders that your pet is managing very well without you can be very upsetting.

Shandy was a small terrier living with his elderly owner in a small block of flats. Often they would sit together in the communal gardens watching the world go by. One afternoon Shandy suddenly leapt up and pounced on a cat, luckily the cat escaped. No one saw the incident except the owner but she was so upset that she resolved there and then to rehome him. She rang a dog rescue society, was told it would probably take months to find him a new home, and then settled down to wait.

Within days the society found Shandy a new home and with scarcely time to reconsider her decision his owner found herself driving him to his new home.

When she arrived she found that his new owners were kind and sensible and lived in a big house with lots of garden. She unloaded his bed and toys and was dismayed when these were consigned to the garage in favour of new ones specially bought for him. She told them about his special diet but they weren't very interested. Now she gets regular letters telling how well he's getting on and how happy he is.

'It seems as though he is happy, he must be with so much freedom, but I am not.'

It quickly becomes clear that the owner has been reduced to the role of spectator, no longer taking part in the decision-making. You might, for example be informed if your former pet becomes ill but you can't help nurse it back to health, you can't take it to the vet you trust, you can't be there when it dies and above all you can't say a final goodbye. In this situation, the owner has to grieve twice, once for the loss of the pet and again when it dies.

Rehoming is not always the end of the story or the end of the sadness that owners have to endure. If you have to rehome a pet you should consider trying to make a clean break. Letters describing a pet's progress are kindly meant but they may prolong your sadness. Owners must decide for themselves what might suit them best.

❏ Going abroad

A common reason for rehoming a pet is if the owner has to go abroad to work. There are many laws controlling the import and export of pet animals, laws intended to prevent the spread of infectious diseases from one country to another.

Whilst it is relatively easy to export dogs and cats *from* the UK, any dog or cat entering the country currently has to be isolated in a licensed quarantine kennel for six months, principally to prevent the importation of rabies. For older pets, six months is a significant part of their remaining life span and it may be impractical or uneconomic to place an old pet in quarantine.

For any pet six months is a long time and kennelling and keep are bound to prove expensive. Added to this are the costs of transport, vaccinations, tests and obtaining the paperwork. For these reasons, going abroad poses major problems for owners of elderly pets or owners whose foreign postings are relatively brief.

❏ Divorce

The problem of what to do with a jointly-owned pet when a relationship breaks up can prove troublesome. If both parties wish to keep the pet, it makes sense, if that is possible, for them to sit down and discuss the following points:

- Who is capable of providing the best care
- Who has sufficient time to exercise the pet
- Who is best able financially to provide the basic needs such as food and vet's bills
- Whether the pet is likely to pine for one more than the other
- Whether it is possible to share the care

One couple who divorced quite amicably, decided on the joint custody of their son *and* their dog! The dog stays with whichever owner is able to provide the best care at that time. It never has to go into kennels, is regularly exercised and, perhaps best of all, their son has been able to maintain his relationship with the pet.

The breakup of relationships is rarely this amicable, however, and when the question of what to do with a pet cannot be settled peacefully, it may be a good idea to approach a counsellor to see if a suitable solution can be mediated.

Losing a pet can be more upsetting than losing a partner. This was discovered by one young man who, although he accepted that his relationship with his live-in girlfriend was over, was extremely distressed by her decision to take both 'their' dogs with her.

She had actually bought the dogs, so rightfully they were hers. However, over the two years of their relationship he had developed a special relationship with them. Years later he still vividly recalls the pain if losing them. 'I didn't mind her going; it was the dogs that I really missed.'

❏ A change of lifestyle

A change in personal circumstances can force an owner to rehome a pet. Many couples acquire a pet when they first set up home together, often as a prelude to starting a family. When children arrive the pet may be unwanted or appear to pose a threat to them; the safety of small children has to be given a higher priority than continued pet ownership.

People who own a pet before they find a partner sometimes find that their pet becomes jealous of the interloper, to the extent of preventing the couple sharing the same bed! The break up of a marriage may also force the rehoming of a family pet. In these instances, grieving by one or both partners can be particularly intense.

Moving

Moving house may mean that a pet has to be found a new home. Some homes are suitable for pets and some are not, some leases allow pets and others do not. Leaving the countryside to live in a town may leave a pet unable to cope with such a radical change of lifestyle. Making the decision in such circumstances, especially if the pet is only middle-aged, can be particularly difficult and upsetting.

Old age

The elderly may be forced to part with their pets if they move into sheltered accommodation. This can be particularly traumatic because the loss of the pet compounds their loss of independence. Fortunately, in recent years the value of pets to the elderly has been recognised and as a result some residential homes have relaxed their rules on the keeping of pets.

Finances

A person's financial position can change for the worse and although pets are important, even essential, in many ways they are really luxury items that need feeding when they are well and expensive veterinary treatment when they are ill. Owners may then have little choice but to take the painful decision to part with their pet.

Health

Some pet owners are advised to rehome their pets for health reasons. Dogs and cats can be implicated in a number of allergic diseases especially asthma and eczema. In some cases doctors will advise patients that these allergies will be alleviated if they 'get rid' of their pets. Even if a person is not specifically allergic to dogs or cats, most allergies have a number of causes and the presence of a dog or cat in the home can make them worse.

In the end the patient has to choose between the inconvenience and discomfort of the allergy and the distress that giving up the pet would bring. In practice many doctors find that their advice is not acted upon, even if the allergy is life threatening.

If the pet is a family pet, the need to rehome it can cause tension within the family. The patient is made to feel guilty and may be the object of blame from other family members for the loss of their pet.

Summary

1. Whether a pet has gone missing or has been rehomed, the owner will need time for adjustment.
2. One of the worst aspects of losing a pet is the uncertainty of its fate.
3. A missing pet is a family problem; face it as a family.
4. Try as hard as possible to find your pet.
5. If, after a few weeks, it has not returned, accept that it is permanently lost to you.
6. Consider holding some form of memorial/ funeral service as a way of recognising your loss.
7. Always ensure that your pet can be identified.
8. Rehousing can be as distressing as any other form of loss.

Chapter 9

Filling the gap

Never another pet for me!
Let your place all vacant be;
Better blankness day by day
Than companion torn away.
Better bid his memory fade,
Better blot each mark he made,
Selfishly escape distress
By contrived forgetfulness,
Than preserve his prints to make
Each morn and eve an ache.

             Thomas Hardy, Last words to a dumb friend

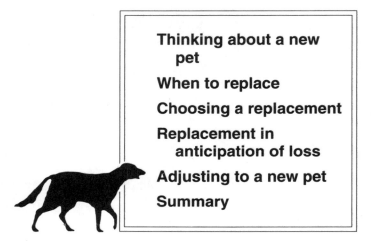

Thinking about a new pet

When to replace

Choosing a replacement

Replacement in anticipation of loss

Adjusting to a new pet

Summary

Thinking about a new pet

Whilst this chapter is all about 'replacing' a dead pet it is obvious that a dearly loved pet cannot simply be replaced like a broken plate. In this context we are using the word to mean the introduction of a new pet after a loss.

Losing a pet is traumatic; mourning for its loss necessarily includes adjusting to life without the pet. Consciously or unconsciously a decision will gradually be made as to whether or not to replace it. The decision isn't always simple; there are many factors to take into consideration.

In the days following the loss many people are convinced that they won't get another because the pain they are suffering seems too much to bear and to risk going through again.

As the grief begins to resolve, many people do start to contemplate the possibility of replacing their pet: this may be days, weeks, or even years after the death. In most cases it is better to attempt to come to terms with your loss before you make a final decision about replacement.

Many people desperately miss owning a pet but worry about their ability to love a new pet as much as the old one. Some people, especially after a very close relationship with a pet, think that they have used up all their love. You can do no more than trust your feelings. If you think you've come to terms with the reality of your pet's death, if you feel you're coping with your grief and you miss the companionship of a pet, then you are probably ready to search for a suitable replacement.

If the dead pet was very much a family pet then there are other people's feelings to take into consideration — especially those of children. Other family members may want another pet even if you don't. If they acquire a replacement you may find that it takes you a long time before you begin to love it. The relationship you shared with your previous pet took years to develop and so will any new relationship.

A number of people experience mixed feelings about becoming a pet owner again, especially if they didn't really want a pet in the first place. Some people are given pets they don't really want and, although they love them, care for them and grieve for their deaths, they don't want to repeat the experience.

One lady was given a kitten, Ellie, as a retirement present. She'd never had a pet before and she didn't want this one. But she took Ellie home and rapidly became very attached to her. When Ellie died she didn't replace her because she'd loved her as an individual, not because she liked cats.

Ultimately, in order to find a successful replacement, you have to loosen the emotional ties with your dead pet. This is in no way a betrayal of its memory, as one owner described.

'I hesitated for a long time before getting another cat; I felt that I would be betraying my dead cat's memory. It was as if he had meant so little to me that I could simply choose another. In truth my previous cat had carved himself an eternal place in my heart and the new one hasn't changed that at all. My dead cat continues to exist alongside my new one.'

Or, as another owner said 'I'm beginning to think about getting another kitten. Although I feel that I would be betraying my cat's memory. I feel that I would only want a replica of her.'

Every animal is a unique individual and as such cannot be replaced but it is possible to replace the essential 'dogness' or 'catness' which made that pet become so important to you. Each animal has a special character that can't be replaced, but most animals can fulfil the basic needs that caused us to become pet owners in the first place.

Even if you have many pets the loss of one particular one can be very painful and may leave a gap that needs to be filled.

❏ The decision not to replace

There are many valid reasons why a bereaved pet owner will choose not to get a new pet. If someone decides not to replace a pet, we should respect their wishes and not attempt to dissuade them or force new pets upon them.

Sometimes the animal may have had a special link with somebody important in the owner's life. It might have been a gift from a dear friend or perhaps might have been the companion of a deceased spouse. In these circumstances the pet might have become so 'special' to the owner that they couldn't ever recapture this with another pet – they are content to live with their memories.

Even when a pet dies of old age and the death was largely expected, an owner can be put off getting another pet because of the emotional strain of watching the pet become ill and slowly fail. 'I think the monthly trips to the vet's for eight months prior to her death were a dreadful strain as I expected each trip to be her last. My health suffered with the stress. I can't face having another pet as I dread the thought of having to go through it all again.'

Some bereaved pet owners express doubt about their ability to form relationships with new pets in the shadow of their pet's death. 'I don't feel able to go through the experience of losing a special pet again and I don't think any other dog would mean the same to me.' 'I never want another dog, I loved her.'

You may decide never to have another pet before your present one dies, anticipating your pain in advance. 'When my last dog dies I will not have any more, it is too painful for me when they die. Their memories will live on and continue to make me smile.'

There are not only emotional reasons for not replacing a pet. Many things may have changed since you first became a pet owner. Some young couples acquire a pet soon after they start a home together because they feel a need to share in the care of a living creature. By the time of the pet's death they may have produced a family and no longer require a pet to fulfil their needs.

Most pets are found in families with children; as time passes and the children grow up and leave home the need to replace a pet may disappear. Other changes of circumstance, like a move to different accommodation or to a different area, may also make people decide not to replace a pet.

Some owners may want to replace a pet but find that the decision has been taken away from them. One such person was an elderly lady living in sheltered housing. When she moved in she was allowed to keep her dog; when it died she wasn't allowed to replace it.

Divorce is another common reason for not replacing a dead pet. There may not be anyone at home all day to look after a new pet which might be young and unable to be left on its own whilst the owner is at work.

For some, cost is a major consideration. Pets cost a lot of money to buy, feed and maintain. An owner may no longer feel able to afford a new pet especially as the first year of pet ownership is usually the most expensive: a new pet must be purchased, vaccinated and probably neutered.

It is particularly sad that many bereaved pet owners decide not to acquire a new pet because of their age. Elderly people often decide not to have a new pet, usually for two main reasons. Firstly they don't relish the thought of trying to train a new pet, especially a young animal that would be too energetic and strong for them to cope with. Secondly many elderly people fear that a pet would outlive them and face an uncertain future.

In many cases there may well be a way around these problems – perhaps by adopting an older pet or sharing a pet, as described below.

❏ The decision to replace

In time most people want to get another pet and indeed do so eventually. In an American survey 85% of people adopting a dog or cat at an animal rescue centre had in fact owned an animal before.

Most people acquire another pet because they miss having an animal about: the companionship, the affection, the security and the need to care for it. In effect the same basic needs they had when they got their first pet still apply. When a pet dies these needs don't die with it and most pet owners feel the need to recreate a similar relationship.

One couple told us: 'In 40 years of married life we had only been without a dog for one week, until two years ago. When we lost two dogs within a year we decided not to get another pet. We wanted to enjoy being free of the responsibility of ownership. My husband became depressed and quite ill. After six months we decided to go out and get another dog. Within a few weeks my husband was back to his old self.'

In the end a pet was such an integral part of this couple's life that they were unable to adapt to life without one.

❏ Pets as presents

Although pets do make delightful presents, they should never be given as 'surprise' gifts; the intended owner may not be ready or simply not want another pet. When one young man presented his parents with a Yorkshire terrier puppy, complete with basket and toys, he was extremely upset when his father told him that they wanted to return the dog to the breeder. His parents simply did not want another dog.

If you want to give a pet as a present, ask the potential owner first. Sharing the decision on species, breed and planning when the new pet can be collected can all add to the pleasure of giving.

❏ Pet sharing

The desire for contact with an animal can be overwhelming and one's life can seem very empty without a pet. A vet and his wife who found themselves in this situation came up with a solution that suited their whole family perfectly. When they lost Anna, a beautiful, loving dobermann, they decided that she was just too special to replace, but they longed for contact with a dog.

After a while, they helped their son and his wife to choose a dog, and now have regular access to this pet. They look after it at holiday times and the dog comes to visit at weekends; they are free from the ultimate responsibilities of pet ownership and their dobermann has not been 'replaced' in their hearts. Their son and his family are also happy with the arrangements knowing that their pet will always be well cared for and will never have to go into kennels if they go away.

When to replace

Every owner is different, every pet is different and so there is no proper time to replace. Everyone must do what is best for them. The important thing is that the result must be a success as far as the owner and the new pet are concerned.

In broad terms, it is easier to form an attachment to your new pet if you are able to loosen the emotional ties with your previous one. In order to do this you must accept the fact that your precious pet can never return. This acceptance doesn't mean that you will forget your fond memories – they will always have a niche in your heart – but that you can start to look towards the future.

This is the theory, but in fact many people rush out and buy a new pet more or less immediately to take their minds off their loss rather than face up to it. Some people do this successfully, some not.

Generally speaking it is unwise to replace a pet before you have had time to accept its death, because you may experience difficulties accepting the replacement.

There are however certain people who need to replace a pet straight away. These include blind people who lose a guide dog, and those who rely on their pet for their livelihood e.g. shepherds and professional dog handlers. Also included in this group are those people, often living alone, who rely very heavily or exclusively on their pet for emotional support and those childless couples for whom the pet is a genuine child substitute. The loss of their pet leaves them so completely alone that the need to have another pet outweighs any possible drawbacks. Typical comments heard in this respect are:

'Although it may sound callous the only way I could cope with the emptiness in my life was to replace her the following day.'

'After a mere three weeks, with what may seem indecent haste, we paid a visit to the breeders. The new dog was my salvation, for without her I fear I would have had some kind of breakdown.'

'The grief I had for Lucy lasted many months but attending to Annie certainly eased the pain. I did not feel as if I was being disrespectful to Lucy because I was giving the love that Lucy should have had to another cat that was much in need of it.'

Unfortunately not everyone has a good experience of rapid replacement. One lady lost a pet Yorkshire terrier after nine years of devoted friendship. Her husband went straight out and bought a golden retriever puppy .

'This was very much against my wishes' she said, 'and I resented the new dog for five years simply because I felt that I was not allowed to mourn for my little Sammy.'

When this couple had lost dogs in the past they had agreed on a two month waiting period before they got another one. For some reason her husband had neglected to consult her about either the time of the replacement or the choice of breed.

Some parents believe that it is beneficial to replace children's pets straight away, that a new pet will help the children forget the old one. Children need just as much time as adults to mourn for their pets and they should be consulted as to their wishes whenever possible.

If your previous pet died of an illness, rather than of old age or an accident you should ask your vet if there is any chance of the disease remaining in the house and re-infecting a new pet. While most diseases don't persist long afterwards some, for example canine parvovirus infection, will persist for several years under certain conditions.

Choosing a replacement

When a pet dies the person looking for a replacement is not the same person that took the puppy or kitten home 15 years previously. So much may have changed or happened in the interim: marriage, children, divorce, widowhood; and there are many factors to consider in the choice: species, breed, age and sex.

Species
Most people remain loyal to a species; dog owners tend to remain dog owners, cat owners mostly remain loyal to cats. The breed of your new pet requires careful consideration. You should consider what your needs are with regard to its character, the amount of exercise and grooming it may need and the cost of its purchase and maintenance. Something else to consider is whether it would get on with any other animals in your house.

Breed

Many people will replace their dead pet with one of the same breed. This seldom causes problems as long as you don't keep comparing the newcomer with its predecessor, looking for deficiencies. Someone who replaced a German shepherd dog with a Cairn terrier found it rather difficult to adapt.

'Although I was very happy with my Cairn puppy it has taken me quite a while to really love him. I expected such a lot from him: I would walk quickly forgetting that he had such little legs.'

Laura, the grand-daughter of the vet mentioned earlier who shares a pet with his son's family, said when the new mongrel was brought home: 'But it's not an Annie dog!' Now she loves the newcomer, Cassie, but not quite as deeply as her sister, Nicole, who never really knew Anna the dobermann.

Some bereaved owners return to the breeder of the dead pet and try to acquire a replacement from the same bloodline. Surveys have shown that people who replace a pet during the acute stage of their mourning are much more likely to choose a pet of the same breed and sex, often giving it the same name. Unfortunately people who do this are often disappointed because no pet is a carbon copy of another no matter how closely they are related.

Two days after the death of her dog one lady went out and bought as exact a replacement as possible, but admitted later: 'I can't love him the way that I loved Henry'.

Age

The former pet's age is also a consideration; barring tragic accidents, most pets die in later life, and it is important to consider whether you feel able to cope with the problems of training a new puppy or would prefer to adopt an older trained dog.

'I was persuaded to get a puppy almost immediately,' one owner told us. 'This is not a move I would advise: after being accustomed to a sedate old dog, a bouncy puppy was almost unbearable.'

As another commented: 'Whilst I looked after the new kitten well, for a while there was no love at all. I didn't want a silly fluffy kitten, I wanted my sleek handsome boy'.

Sex

The sex of your new pet may not be much of a problem as all pets can be neutered if necessary to control their breeding. If , however, you have other pets of the same species you should choose the replacement's sex with care; males may fight and male and female animals will inevitably breed unless closely controlled.

More than one

It's not unusual for owners to get more than one replacement as an 'insurance policy' against being left without a pet again. They're hoping that they can dilute their attachment and reduce their pain when one of the pets dies. The reality, though, is that we become attached to pets as individuals and grieve just as much when one of them dies. The main drawback of owning two pets of the same age is that they might both die of old age at about the same time, making your grief greater not smaller.

Replacement in anticipation of loss

Some pet owners acquire a new pet when their existing pet starts to become old or ill. They hope that forming a relationship with their new pet will help them to cope with the death of the first one. The relationship between the owner and the new pet should give comfort to the owner at the time of loss, but must never be used to avoid grieving.

Forming a relationship with a new pet may help children to cope with the impending death of a long standing family pet. They can turn to the new pet for consolation when they are feeling sad about the loss of their loyal companion.

The decision to find a replacement can cause disputes at home: some may not want a replacement, others may not want to admit that the pet is dying.

It is important to consider what effect the introduction of a new pet will have on an old or ill animal. Your main consideration has to be the care and welfare of your first pet, the last thing an ill dog may need is to be pestered by a puppy. You have to have enough time to look after the old pet properly and should consider whether the old pet is likely to resent the intrusion of a newcomer on its territory.

In many ways anticipated replacement is not fair on the new pet, because the owner may find it difficult to form a relationship with it whilst the old pet is still living. 'Buying another pet to replace Mandy before she died did little good. The quality of my relationship with the new dog simply did not compare with that of my relationship with Mandy.'

Points to consider when contemplating obtaining a replacement pet

● Have you finished grieving for your dead pet?
● Are you looking for another pet or simply a reincarnation of your dead pet?
● Do you feel able to treat a new pet as a separate entity not just a continuation of your previous pet?
● Do you feel that you simply can't live without a pet in your life?
● Are your pet-related needs the same as when you acquired your previous pet? Do you still have a need to be filled?
● Having had a time free from the responsibility of owning a pet are you sure that you want the responsibility again?
● Have your domestic arrangements changed, or are they going to change in the near future, making it prudent to delay a decision to replace?
● Have your financial circumstances changed so that a new pet may not be practical?
● Have you remembered how much exercise a younger pet may need?
● Have you considered the needs and wishes of other family members?

Adjusting to a new pet

The first months after you acquire a new pet can be critical. You should be prepared to accept the pet as an individual character and not be tempted to make comparisons between it and the previous pet. Don't expect too much too soon, it may take years for attachments to develop, you can't pick up the new relationship where the old one finished.

FILLING THE GAP

Your new pet will need time to get to know you too. Initially it won't obey you or anticipate your wishes like your old pet could.

You can expect to find a lot of differences between an old pet and its young replacement; it will be boisterous, maybe destructive and it may not want to spend as much time sitting on your knee or by your side.

When you welcome a new pet into your home you're not being disloyal to the memory of your previous pet, rather your new pet is a tribute to its memory because your experience of successful ownership has encouraged you to become a pet owner again. Take time to think about your dead pet, allow its memory to 'live' alongside your love for your new pet.

Remember that other family members will adjust to the new pet at different speeds. The other animals in your house may also take some time to adjust to the newcomer. Your pets may feel threatened by the arrival of a new pet and jealous of the fuss that is made of it. Dogs are social animals but they maintain a rigid pack structure; the arrival of a new pet – it doesn't even have to be a dog – can cause considerable upheaval, even fighting. Cats are not social animals but like to maintain personal territories; putting a new cat into another's territory can cause friction initially.

Summary

1. Just as there is no set time for grieving, there is no right time for getting another pet. The decision to get another pet is extremely personal and only you will know if you're really ready and able to take on a new pet.
2. Most people know instinctively whether they want a new pet or not. Others need to take time to make up their minds. Even if you make a decision soon after the death of your pet it is generally best to allow some time to pass before you actually acquire your new one so that you are ready to accept it into your heart as well as your home.
3. There is no disgrace in getting a new pet quickly if you feel that it would help you to recover from your loss, or if you simply feel lost without an animal in your life.
4. If you really think that you are unable to form a relationship with your new pet you should consider finding it a new home rather than persevering with an animal you resent.
5. If you decide not to get another pet it is important that other people are aware of, and respect, that decision. This avoids the possibility of you being presented with a puppy or kitten as a 'surprise'.
6. If it is possible don't deny yourself the opportunity to love, and be loved by, another pet if that is what you really want. There is no better tribute to your previous pet than your willingness and readiness to start a new relationship.

Chapter 10

Do pets grieve?

Hast thou longed through weary days
For the sight of one loved face.

William Morris, Love fulfilled, A book of verse

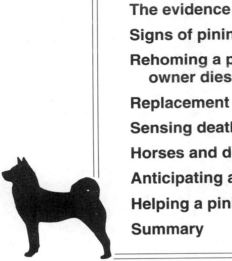

The evidence

Signs of pining

Rehoming a pet when its owner dies

Replacement

Sensing death

Horses and donkeys

Anticipating animal grief

Helping a pining animal

Summary

The evidence

We all know that owners grieve when a pet dies, but what happens when a pet loses its owner, or loses a close animal companion? Does it grieve as well?

It is obvious that animals can experience hunger, fear and pain, but can they experience a sense of loss? No-one knows what goes on inside an animal's head but animals certainly show changes in their behaviour patterns when they lose a close animal or human companion.

An animal may not be able to realise that its companion or owner is dead in the way we can, but it will certainly react to the fact that something is missing.

119

DO PETS GRIEVE?

It would be unwise to attribute human emotions and thoughts to our pets but many phenomena have been recorded that can't be explained in terms of simple loss.

The most famous historical example of a pet apparently mourning is that of Greyfriars Bobby who, in 1858, 'followed the remains of his master to Greyfriars' churchyard and lingered near the spot until his own death in 1872'. In reality Greyfriars Bobby did not spend those 14 years at the graveside, but he did live locally and was fed by various people including the soldiers at the nearby Edinburgh Castle. He seemed to know where his master was buried, was often found at the grave and he did have to be forcibly moved occasionally.

A similar story that we came across was that of Corrie, a chocolate labrador bitch whose mistress died one February. Corrie became very distressed and by June she was so ill that she was taken to see a vet. Despite numerous tests a diagnosis was never made and Corrie died in September. Even a post-mortem examination didn't reveal the cause of death. Her owner, who had lost his wife and his dog within seven months of each other could only conclude that Corrie had lost the will to live.

Fortunately, although many animals do experience behavioural changes when they lose a companion, the vast majority recover and resume normal lives.

Signs of pining

- Loss of appetite
- Lethargy
- Aimless pacing around the house or garden
- Apparent searching for their absent companion
- Changes in sleeping patterns and an inability to settle properly
- Disinterest in exercise
- Crying at night
- Self-mutilation (this is more common in cats)

These signs are seen if the pet is separated from its owner or companion even for only short periods of time. Naturally the pet doesn't know how long the separation will last and usually the acute signs of anxiety subside after a few days.

In reality very few pets pine to death.

Rehoming a pet when an owner dies

When an owner dies or becomes unable to look after a pet, the pet may have to be rehomed and this can prove difficult for both the pet and the new owner. Dogs often adapt quite well to a new environment and, although there will be a time of adjustment whilst the animal settles down to a new routine and a new owner, the new environment may well help the dog to get over his pining for his previous owner.

In contrast cats tend to become closely bonded to one individual and if that individual dies they may find it very difficult to adjust, becoming introverted and changing their behaviour quite markedly.

'She always remained my mother's cat,' the new owner of a rehomed cat told us.

Eventually the cat may form a bond with its new owner but it takes time and patience: old cats are much more set in their ways and therefore have much more difficulty settling down.

Replacement

A dog is also much more likely to accept a replacement after its companion dies than a cat would be. Some cats never really accept a replacement for the companion they grew up with; it may take many months or it may never happen. Many cats simply behave as if the replacement does not exist.

The decision to replace a pet must be based on your own personal feelings and also on your assessment of how a replacement would affect your existing pets.

In some cases a replacement pet has proved positively beneficial. Brammer, a labrador cross, and Bungle, a beagle, were inseparable. When Brammer became ill and euthanasia was carried out, Bungle appeared to become very depressed. Although he would show an interest in other dogs out on his walks, at home he was listless and miserable. After a year his owner acquired Bobby, another beagle, and after a period of adjustment Bungle is more or less back to normal.

Although many animals show a change of behaviour following the death of a companion, not all changes are adverse ones. The death of a dominant pet may allow its more submissive companion to 'blossom'; a shy, nervous cat may become confident and affectionate, a submissive dog may become the 'leader of the pack'. When the 'leader of the pack' in a household of dogs dies, a new leader has to emerge and this may initially cause friction until the new social order becomes established.

Sensing death

The warden of a block of flats agreed to look after an elderly lady's dog when she went into hospital. At 11am one morning, for no apparent reason the dog sat up and howled. A little while later the hospital rang to say the lady had passed away – at 11am!

In Taiwan many people ask a priest to visit when they hear a dog howl, because a family death is believed to be imminent.

Even in the fictional Sherlock Holmes stories, the howling of a hound announced the imminent death of a member of the Baskerville family.

Tales of this nature are so numerous that it is hard to separate fact from fiction. It is not possible to reach any definite conclusion on the awareness of animals, but it is acceptable to suppose that animals may have faculties beyond our comprehension.

Horses and donkeys

Horses and, more especially, donkeys can form deep and lasting attachments with their companions. Following the loss of a companion they can show a variety of behavioural changes including loss of appetite, listlessness and refusal to leave their stables.

Sally, a donkey, and Winston, a pony, had lived together for many years before they finally came to live at a horse sanctuary near Lincoln. Wherever Winston went, Sally followed. They lived alone and refused to mix with the other horses. When Winston died, Sally refused to eat and stayed in her stable all day. After six weeks she was moved into a yard near where people walked and close to other donkeys. Gradually she started eating again and eventually found a new companion – Joshua, a goat!

In the case of donkeys, and possibly other domestic species, it is generally accepted that it is beneficial to allow the surviving partner to see the body of its companion. This is thought to reduce the duration and severity of the distress they suffer.

Anticipating animal grief

If it is obvious that two animals are deeply attached to one another, and you are aware that shortly one of them will die, there are several things you can do to help shorten and reduce the distress experienced by the survivor.

Before its partner dies, introduce the pet to changes in its daily routine; if the animals have always fed together, stagger their meal times so that they get used to eating on their own, or in the presence of other animals. By doing this you are trying to break the dependency that one animal has on the other. Pining animals may refuse to eat because the right conditions are not present, i.e. their companion is absent.

It can also help to introduce a pet to other animals before its companion dies. Again this may reduce the dependency that one has on the other. With dogs it often works well to introduce a younger dog so that the remaining dog will begin to form a relationship, and learn to eat with it before its companion dies.

Heidi is a nine-year-old German shepherd dog who lives with Vita, her daughter. The two dogs are inseparable and Vita displays acute anxiety when they are separated. Recently, Heidi was discovered to have lung cancer and possibly no more than three months to live. After consulting her vet, the owner decided to buy a German shepherd puppy, Asta, who settled down well with the two older dogs. Vita has another dog to romp around with, which gives Heidi chance to rest. The hope is that when Heidi eventually dies, the bond between Vita and Asta will be strong enough to prevent Vita from pining for her.

Helping a pining pet

If the animal will not eat and seems totally disinterested in life a visit to the veterinary surgery may be helpful. Your vet will check your pet over for any physical illness which could be the underlying cause of the problem and may be able to give your pet something to encourage it to eat.

A change of location may help the animal to establish new habits and thus help it to adjust to life without its companion.

As mentioned before, some animals benefit from a new companion, and this is especially true of dogs. Some dogs will take readily to a young puppy as a new companion, but older dogs may not be able to tolerate the antics of such a young dog. Your vet may well be the best person to advise you on the particular breed and age of a replacement pet.

Counselling help from an animal behaviourist is available if you have long-term problems with a pining animal. All animals are individuals; whereas one animal may respond to one particular form of therapy, another may need something quite different. Talking with an animal behaviourist may well be the best means of establishing the correct way to treat your pet's particular problems.

Summary

1. When an animal dies, other animals in the household will show behavioural changes. Occasionally an animal will be seriously affected.
2. Some pining animals benefit from the introduction of a replacement companion.
3. If you think your pet will pine, consider introducing a new pet in anticipation of loss.
4. Dogs are much more adaptable than cats.
5. Consult your vet if signs of pining persist. It may be necessary, in extreme cases, to seek help from an animal behaviourist.

Chapter 11

Obituaries

We've sorrow enough in the natural way,
When it comes to burying Christian clay.
Our loves are not given, but only lent,
At compound interest of cent per cent.
Though it is not always the case, I believe,
That the longer we've kept 'em, the more do we grieve,
For, when debts are payable, right or wrong,
A short time loan is as bad as a long
So why in Heaven (before we are there)
Should we give our hearts to a dog to tear?

  Rudyard Kipling, The Power of the Dog

Junior, a precious little cat

Tanya, the gentle giant

Amber, a dream come true

Mark and Butch

Benson, my alter ego

Vanessa and Cassie

Junior, a precious little cat

Junior, a tiny lilac point Siamese kitten, was 11 months old when he became ill with severe kidney disease. The vet suggested euthanasia to Gabrielle, his breeder, but she looked at her frail white kitten and sensed that his pale blue eyes were willing her to fight for him.

Gabrielle began a devoted regime of 24-hour nursing. She would wrap him in a blanket and carry him round the house, showing him the trees through the windows hoping that one day he would have the strength to climb them. The intensive nursing seemed to revive Junior and for a while he seemed like his old self.

But, several months later, he became ill again. Death seemed inevitable but Gabrielle kept on fighting to save him. Junior was now being fed with a syringe and he weighed only 12 pounds. The vet again suggested euthanasia but Gabrielle refused to give in.

A month later, all Gabrielle's efforts were rewarded; Junior walked unaided into the kitchen and started to eat. The vet was amazed when, as the weeks went by, Junior went from strength to strength. Gabrielle was unable to believe her eyes the day she saw a proud Junior sitting on a branch in the apple tree, and she ran to fetch her camera to record this longed for moment. At last Gabrielle felt that she had been right to fight for her beloved little cat.

When Junior was almost two years old, builders working in the house left a door open and Junior wandered out onto the road. He was killed not 50 yards from the front gate. On Gabrielle's return home a tearful neighbour handed her a bundle wrapped in a blanket.

Gabrielle was overwhelmed with grief and anger. It seemed so unfair that after all her efforts, Junior's life should be cut short, so tragically, by means beyond her control.

As the weeks passed into months her grief deepened but she was unable to confide in anyone, not even her husband. The only thing she could compare her emotions to was the grief she had experienced four years previously when her father died; the anger, guilt, sadness and hopelessness were the same. Gabrielle felt it was somehow wrong to feel the same emotions for her cat. It was only after contacting a pet loss adviser that she began to realise just how normal her reactions to Junior's death were. She experienced a great sense of relief and stopped trying to deny her intense grief. In time she began to explain to others how she felt.

Gabrielle dreads Junior's birthday and the anniversary of his death as she knows that these will be difficult days to face. She had owned Junior for only two years but it had seemed like an eternity to her. Gabrielle still grieves for her father but now she also feels that she has the permission she needs to grieve for Junior, a precious family member, a precious little cat.

Tanya, the gentle giant

It was October 1985 when Richard decided to look for an Old English Sheepdog as a Christmas present for his wife. He contacted the Old English Sheepdog rescue society and almost immediately was offered a three-and-a-half year old bitch.

Tanya made an immediate and immense impression on everyone and she soon became an important member of the family. She was huge, over seven stone, with a character even larger than life. She settled in well and soon made it clear that it was she that had adopted the family. She took immediate charge of the family including Baron, the Airedale, who made an early decision to give in gracefully.

In August 1988 they all went on a canal boat holiday and during this time Tanya started to look ill. When they returned home their vet diagnosed a fatal form of cancer and gave her about a month to live.

On the 23rd of December, a time when most families are coming together to celebrate Christmas, Richard was faced with the most difficult decision of his life. He realised that Tanya's time had come and so he arranged for the vet to carry out euthanasia. The pain of that decision still stays with him, even though he knew that he was doing the kindest thing possible in releasing Tanya from her pain.

In the months that followed they consoled themselves by watching video recordings of Tanya, made when she was full of life and bursting with energy. Richard believes that his house is more beautiful for having photographs of Tanya on the walls and that his family is richer for having known, loved and lost Tanya, the larger than life Old English Sheepdog who adopted a family in Taunton.

Amber, a dream come true

Ever since Donna saw *Lady and the Tramp* she had longed for a dogl of her own. Her dream came true when her mother presented her with a beautiful puppy. Donna, who was 19, called the puppy Amber and over the next nine years she developed a deep and loving relationship with her.

A few years later Donna's mother died and she turned again to Amber for comfort. Amber became even more important to Donna because she had been a gift from her mother.

Not long after this her father died. Donna felt very alone and she turned again to Amber for help through the dismal, depressing months that followed. It seemed that Amber was the only 'family' she had left.

In June 1986 Donna realised that Amber was unwell. A vet initially diagnosed a chest infection but unfortunately complications developed. Amber didn't seem to respond to treatment at home and appeared very listless. The vet was, however, optimistic and everyone hoped that Amber would pick up.

A month later, at 4.15pm, Amber let out one small woof, collapsed and died.

Donna suffered from severe shock and the pain she felt was as deep as when her mother had died. She became depressed, felt totally alone, and even contemplated suicide. She was aware that sympathetic people thought it was sad that she had lost her dog, but she had lost much more than that and she couldn't cope with the embarrassment of people who were unable to comprehend her grief.

It's nearly five years since Amber died, but whenever Donna sees a golden Cocker Spaniel in the street she goes over to it and touches it, recapturing for a second the wonderful warmth of Amber.

Mark and Butch

This is a story that includes both human and pet loss. Mark's parents would like his story to be told as a tribute to both his and Butch's memory.

Mark was described as a normal, honest sort of person but highly strung with an inability to express or release his innermost feelings. He was very attached to the family pets: Butch the boxer, Petra the Yorkie and Butchie a crossbred.

When Mark left home, his parents thought that he should take Butch with him for company. Mark became very attached to Butch who became the focal point of his life.

The first signs of trouble appeared when Butch became very ill. Unable to cope, Mark spent the night at his parents' house where he took an overdose. Luckily Mark survived but then Butch had to be taken to the vet for euthanasia and from that moment Mark's world ceased to exist. His parents were extremely worried and they tried to help him with his grief but he insisted on going home alone to face his empty house.

At home Mark wrote a note in which he explained how sorry he was for the trouble he would undoubtedly cause but he couldn't live without Butch. Mark was killed the next morning at 7.15am by the Leeds to Knottingly train. His parents were devastated; they had realised that Mark would find it difficult to live without Butch but the shock of his death was a dreadful blow.

To live with the pain of losing a beloved pet was very difficult; to live with the pain of losing a son was almost unbearable.

Since Mark's death both Petra and Butchie have also died and each additional loss brought back the pain of losing Mark and Butch. Sometimes one family can be struck by so much pain and suffering that those who survive are permanently changed. Mark cannot be brought back but his devotion to, and dependence on, Butch will never be forgotten.

Benson, my alter ego

Benson was my own cat. He was big, black and beautiful. It was his sudden death that prompted me, together with my husband, Martyn, to turn my research into a book on pet loss.

I obtained Benson when I was single and living in London. I had just bought a flat, I was penniless and had no furniture so my boss told me that what I really needed to turn my flat into a home was a cat. Benson was the biggest, fluffiest kitten I'd ever seen and I fell for him straight away. He soon settled into my life and became my constant companion.

When I was ill it was Benson who sat on my pillow and shared the grapes; when the phone didn't ring it was Benson who was there to comfort me. I even met my husband through Benson and it wasn't long before Benson had Martyn under his spell too.

It was on Good Friday 1990, when he was nine years old, that I noticed that Benson seemed quiet. He came and sat by me; I had never realised before that he would come to me when he felt ill, although he had always appeared by my side whenever I was unwell.

Martyn took him to his surgery on Saturday and X-rays revealed a large mass in his abdomen. We seemed to have three options: do nothing, treat him with drugs to make him comfortable until he died or operate in the hope of being able to remove the mass completely. I asked what the chances of a successful operation were. Martyn replied: 'No more than 25%'. It wasn't much but Benson had always done his best by me, now I had to do the same for him.

The following morning, Easter Sunday, I drove Benson to the surgery. I held him whilst Martyn anaesthetised him, then I went to wait in the office. It wasn't long before Martyn appeared. His face said it all. I was going to lose my Ben.

I took his body home and just held him. I couldn't believe that he was gone. He had been so much a part of my life and I wasn't ready to let go of him or my memories. We buried him in the garden and planted a tree over his grave.

Martyn chose damsons because, like Benson, they were black on the outside and golden in the middle.

I remember the awful pain that followed. I felt so empty. I felt like I'd lost my right arm. I couldn't remember life without Benson. Eventually I learnt to cope; I faced my grief, vented my anger, confronted my guilt and then dealt with my sorrow. Benson carved a place in my heart and like all special pets he will never be forgotten.

Vanessa and Cassie

Audrey was absolutely delighted when her 14-year-old daughter, Vanessa, saved up all her pocket money to buy a small cross-bred puppy. Vanessa called her Cassie and it wasn't long before they were inseparable and Cassie became well loved by the entire family. As the years passed, Cassie became very definitely Vanessa's dog and so when Vanessa was killed by a drunken driver, Cassie suffered as much as the family.

As Audrey and her family learnt to live with Vanessa's death they were greatly comforted by Cassie's presence. Cassie started to accompany Audrey everywhere as if she, Cassie, was afraid of being left alone, afraid that her owner might not return again. In June 1990, Audrey's husband was out walking with Cassie when she was attacked and killed by two large dogs. Cassie's death was another tragedy for the family. The circumstances of her death echoed those of Vanessa's; it was both senseless and tragic. After a death like this it was hard to find comfort in anything. Cassie had been the last living link with Vanessa: her death undoubtedly renewed the grief that the family had experienced when Vanessa died. For Audrey it was the end of a very special part of her life, now she has only photographs and memories to remind her of a wonderful daughter and a devoted animal companion.

Pet loss – the facts

While a considerable amount of research has been carried out in the UK, especially by members of the Society for Companion Animal Studies, most of the published work is from North America.

Rather than base our book on other people's work, much of which may not be relevant in the UK, we decided to conduct some research of our own.

A detailed questionnaire was drawn up covering most aspects of pet loss. We advertised for volunteers in the pet magazines and this led to an article in the Daily Telegraph which in turn elicited more volunteers. Ultimately we received nearly 1,000 completed questionnaires, mainly from dog and cat owners, but covering the full spectrum of pet ownership from hamsters to horses.

With the help of Dr Douglas Davies of the Department of Theology at the University of Nottingham, all the questionnaires were used to create the data base on which this appendix is based.

1. How old was your pet when it died? (Figures 1 and 2)

Responses to this question showed a marked difference between cats and dogs. Cats appear to be capable of living longer than dogs – 33% of them were over 15 years old when they died, compared to 20% of dogs. Despite this, more dogs live to be over 10 years of age – 72% compared to 58% of cats. It is probable that the difference is due to the much higher risk of a

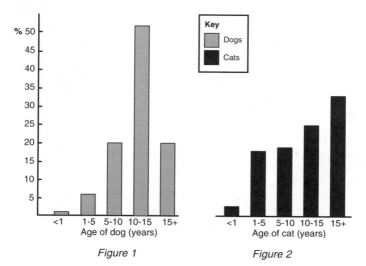

Figure 1   Figure 2

APPENDIX 1

young cat being killed in a road accident (see Figure 3). Future analysis may show if these differences have any bearing on the degree of bereavement experienced by cat and dog owners.

2.   What did your pet die of? (Figure 3)

More cats are killed on the road than dogs, and as a result, a higher proportion of dogs eventually die of old age.

3.   When your pet died, how did you feel? (Figure 4)

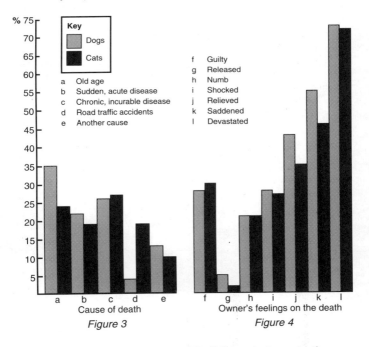

Key	
▨	Dogs
■	Cats

a Old age
b Sudden, acute disease
c Chronic, incurable disease
d Road traffic accidents
e Another cause

f Guilty
g Released
h Numb
i Shocked
j Relieved
k Saddened
l Devastated

Cause of death

Owner's feelings on the death

Figure 3

Figure 4

4.   Did you feel angry when your pet died? If so, at whom was the anger directed? (Figure 5)

Overall 39% of cat owners felt anger on the death of their pet, compared with 28% of dog owners. This is, again, probably accounted for by the higher proportion of cats killed in road accidents. The results shown in figure 5 tend to confirm this view because twice as many cat owners as dog owners felt anger towards the person thought to have caused the death – in most cases the driver of a car. Similarly, more cat owners felt angry that fate, personified by God, had caused their pet to die.

5. Did you consult your family doctor as a consequence of the death of your pet?

10% of those owners completing the questionnaire had consulted their family doctor about their feelings of bereavement. 75% of those who were dog owners and 50% of the cat owners felt that the doctor was sympathetic; but only 49% and 22% respectively found their doctor any specific help.

6. Did you need to take time off work?

13% of dog owners and 18% of cat owners took time off from work as a direct result of their pet's death.

7. Have you been able to fully accept the death of your pet? How long did this take you? (Figure 6)

The time needed for acceptance of the death was very variable. Most owners took months, but a sizeable number took years to come to terms with their loss.

47% of dog owners felt that their pet's death had greatly altered their lives, compared with 38% of cat owners. This may reflect the fact that looking after a dog is a more active process – most dogs require daily walks, etc.

Nearly 80% of dog owners and 75% of cat owners felt that their pet's death was the end of a chapter in their lives. 75% of pet deaths revived memories of previous bereavements, both human and animal.

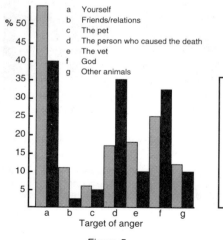

a   Yourself
b   Friends/relations
c   The pet
d   The person who caused the death
e   The vet
f   God
g   Other animals

Target of anger

Figure 5

Time	Dog owners	Cat owners
Days	15%	12%
Weeks	14%	14%
Months	42%	47%
Years	27%	23%

Time for acceptance

Figure 6

APPENDIX 1

8. Did you have to make a decision regarding euthanasia?

Euthanasia had been carried out on 75% of dogs and 63% of cats in this survey.

87% of dog owners who had decided to have euthanasia carried out on their pets would have preferred their pet to have died in its sleep. However, 97% felt they had made the right decision at the time.

Euthanasia had been carried out at home in only 36% of dogs and 26% of cats, despite the fact that 62% of dog owners and 68% of cat owners would have preferred this option. This demonstrates a considerable gap between what people actually want and the service currently offered by vets. In fact, only 37% of dog owners and 30% of cat owners had been offered a choice at all.

77% of dog owners and 66% of cat owners had been present when the euthanasia had been performed; the difference may be accounted for by the fact that euthanasia had been carried out at home on a greater number of dogs.

9. How did you dispose of your pet's remains?

Cats are much more likely to be buried at home; in contrast, dogs are more likely to be disposed of by cremation. This difference is probably a reflection of the practical difficulties that accompany the home burial of larger pets.

Only 2% of dogs and 3% of cats were buried in pet cemeteries, although 42% of dog owners and 33% of cat owners said they would have used a cemetery if one was available.

34% of dogs and 22% of cats were cremated. In each case, approximately one-third of these pets were cremated individually. 29% of dog owners and 20% of cat owners were not sure what happened to their pet's remains, but it is likely that most of these were disposed of by vets, usually by cremation, following euthanasia. It seems that there is an increasing trend towards cremation, with a considerable number of owners choosing individual cremation for their pet.

Although 73% of dog owners and 76% of cat owners were happy about their choice, this leaves a quarter of pet owners who were unhappy with the way in which their pet was disposed of. This may be a reflection of several factors: lack of actual choice, cost, or the difficulty of making a decision at the time of the pet's death. 40% of pet owners had found it difficult to make a reasoned decision at the time.

10. *Have you acquired any other pets since the death of your pet? If so, how long did you wait? (Figure 7)*

Since the death of their pet, 50% of dog owners and 48% of cat owners had acquired a replacement. Dog owners appeared more inclined to get an immediate replacement – perhaps because they tended to have greater emotional dependency on their pet.

Over half of owners took months or years to replace their pet, while only 8% of dog owners and 5% of cat owners acquired another pet before their old pet died.

Of the owners who had not acquired a new pet, the commonest reason was that they were not yet ready, but would probably get another in due course. (Figure 8)

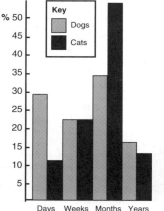

Days Weeks Months Years
Time taken to replace pet

Figure 7

a   Not yet ready
b   Fear of further emotional trauma
c   Owner too old to start again
d   Fear of betraying pet's memory
e   Change of circumstances
f   Don't want responsibility again
g   Other reasons

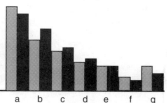

a   b   c   d   e   f   g
Reasons for not acquiring another pet

Figure 8

APPENDIX 1

11. Did you share a special relationship with your pet? (Figure 9)

78% of pet owners felt they shared a special relationship with their pet –
99% regarded their pet as part of the family (see Figure 10).

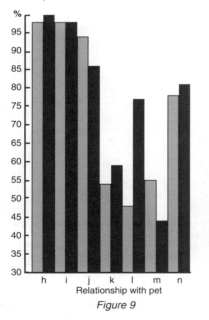

h Did you talk to your pet?
i Were you aware of your pet's moods?
j Was your pet aware of your moods?
k Did you share your food with your pet?
l Did your pet sleep on your bed?
m Did you celebrate your pet's birthday?
n Are you aware of the anniversary of your pet's death?

Relationship with pet

Figure 9

Status in family	Dogs	Cats
An equal adult member	19%	23%
A junior member	25%	25%
An animal member	54%	51%
Other	2%	1%

Status of pet in family

Figure 10

12. Have you kept any mementoes of your pet? (Figure 11)

97% of pet owners had kept some memento of their pet; 89% of these people deriving comfort from them. Of those who had not kept anything, 35% of dog owners and 42% of cat owners wished that they had.

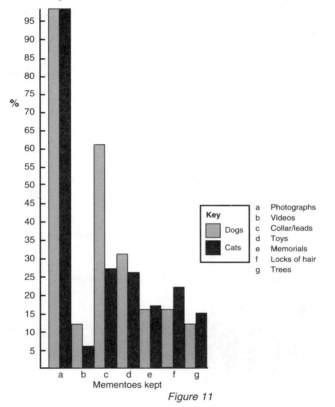

Figure 11

The findings presented here represent just a fraction of the information obtained from our survey, but they serve to illustrate the differing ways in which dog and cat owners relate to the death of their pets. A more detailed analysis, to be published elsewhere, will examine how the age of a pet and the way it died influences grief, and will look more closely at how pet loss affects the elderly and people who live alone. The facts given here should help vets and owners of pet crematoria and cemetaries provide a service better tailored to the needs of bereaved pet owners.

Pet charities

All the societies listed below are registered charities and therefore dependent on donations, subscriptions and legacies for funding their activities.

The Blue Cross

The Blue Cross can provide veterinary services for pets whose owners genuinely cannot afford private veterinary fees. The Blue Cross operates 12 animal welfare centres and four animal hospitals or clinics all over England and a mobile clinic in Dublin.
The Blue Cross, Shilton Road, Burford, Oxon OX8 4PF
Tel: 0993 822651

Cats' Protection League (CPL)

Founded over 60 years ago, the League today has over 200 groups and branches around the country. Their objectives are to rescue stray and unwanted cats and kittens, rehabilitate and rehome them where possible; to encourage the neutering of cats not required for breeding and to inform the public on the care of cats and kittens.
Cats' Protection League, 17 Kings Road, Horsham, West Sussex RH13 5PP
Tel: 0403 61947

The National Canine Defence League (NCDL)

The NCDL was founded over 100 years ago at the first all-breed Crufts dog show. Its remit is the promotion of the welfare of dogs. They aim to find all unwanted dogs caring new owners – those that are not rehomed become permanent residents of their many kennels. The NCDL campaign on a national level on all dog-related subjects. They operate the 'Lucky Dog Club' and identification discs are available though the club.
NCDL, 1 Pratt Mews, London NW1 0AD
Tel: 071 388 0137

The Peoples' Dispensary for Sick Animals (PDSA)

The PDSA has been in operation for over 70 years. They provide a free veterinary service for the sick and injured pets of owners unable to afford private veterinary fees. Owners who are on certain state benefits are eligible for the Society's free service.

The PDSA, PDSA House, Whitechapel Way, Priorslee, Telford TF2 2AQ
Tel: 0952 290999

PRO-Dogs

PRO-Dogs was started in Kent 15 years ago to help pet owners facing problems of any kind. The Pet Aided Therapy (PAT)dog visiting scheme was originated by the organisation in 1983 and there are now 5,700 registered dogs who visit hospitals, hospices and residential homes where people would otherwise be deprived of animal contact. PRO-Dogs has recently started a grief counselling scheme to help those faced with the loss of a pet.

PRO-Dogs, Rocky Bank, 4 New Road, Ditton, Kent ME20 6AD
Tel: 0732 848499

The Royal Society for the Prevention of Cruelty to Animals (RSPCA)

The RSPCA was founded in 1824 to promote kindness and prevent cruelty to animals. It is the world's largest animal welfare organisation and its work in this country is carried out by uniformed inspectors and thousands of volunteers who are based in branches throughout England and Wales.

RSPCA, Causeway, Horsham, West Sussex RH13 1HG
Tel: 0403 64181

The Society for Companion Animal Studies (SCAS)

SCAS was set up in 1979 by a group of doctors, social workers and veterinary surgeons in Britain and the USA to promote interest in human/companion animal relationships. SCAS welcomes members from all walks of life.

SCAS, The Mews Cottage, 7 Botanic Crescent Lane, Glasgow G20 8AA
Tel: 041 945 2088

Wood Green Animal Shelters

The Wood Green Animal Shelter was founded in 1925, primarily to relieve the pain and suffering of abandoned, injured and sick animals. There are now additional centres in Heydon, Godmanchester and King's Bush. Wood Green operate the National Pet Register, a computerised identification system to which there is 24-hour access to trace owners of missing pets.

Wood Green Animal Shelters, Highway Cottage, Chishill Road, Heydon, Royston, Herts SG8 8PN
Tel: 0763 838329

Friskies Petcare Helpline

The Friskies Petcare Helpline is a co-ordinated information and advice service for pet owners, primarily those faced with problems such as what to do when a pet goes missing, or what to do if they find a pet. Details of volunteers can be obtained from the co-ordination office on 071 352 7220.

Friskies Petcare, King's Gate House, 536 Kings Road, London SW10 0TE

Note

Although not charitable organisations, the following offer a telephone advisory service for pet owners in need of support at the time of pet death.

Cambridge Pet Crematorium and CPC Petrest

The Cambridge Pet Crematorium is the UK's largest facility for the cremation of pets – from a hamster to a horse. The gardens of remembrance are open to visitors throughout the year. Owners can also attend and witness the cremation of their pet.

CPC Petrest is the pet funeral service of the crematorium and can offer collection of the pet from home or the vet's surgery. Ashes are returned to owners personally.

Petrest operates a counselling line *(Freephone Petrest)* for owners in need of advice and guidance.

Cambridge Pet Crematorium, A505 Main Road, Thriplow Heath, nr Royston, Herts SG8 7RR   (0763) 208295
CPC Petrest (0763) 248259 or Freephone Petrest